FLIRTING WITH D_____
& SPANKING THE MONKEY

FLIRTING WITH DISASTER
& SPANKING THE MONKEY
David O. Russell

faber and faber
LONDON · BOSTON

All rights reserved under International and Pan-American
Copyright Conventions, including the right of reproduction in
whole or in part in any form.

First published in the United States in 1996
by Faber and Faber Inc.
50 Cross Street, Wincester MA/ 01890
and in the United Kingdom by Faber and Faber Limited
3 Queen Square London WCIN 3AU

Photoset by Parker Typesetting Service, Leicester
Printed in England by Clays Ltd, St Ives plc

David O. Russell is hereby identified as author of this work in accordance with
Section 77 of the Copyright, Designs and Patents Act 1988

A CIP record for this book
is available from The Library of Congress
and from the British Library
ISBN 0-571-19701-5

2 4 6 8 10 9 7 5 3 1

CONTENTS

DAVID O. RUSSELL
FLYING UNDER THE RADAR

David O. Russell was born in Manhattan in 1958 and raised just
north of New York City in suburban Westchester. He took a
roundabout way to becoming a writer–director, as he explains in
the following interview, but with his first two features, *Spanking
the Monkey* (1994) and *Flirting with Disaster* (1996), he has swiftly
emerged as one of the most promising film-makers in America.
What is a David O. Russell film? So far it is hard to say, but
watching one leaves the viewer simultaneously charmed and
discomfited. *Spanking* and *Flirting* are linked by their interest in
the jail of family life, and the misbehavior of the inmates, although
Russell intends to make a different kind of film next time out. The
qualities in his work that should survive the change of tack are the
sharp situational writing, the acute social observation, the
elliptical, intentionally disorienting *mise en scène* and the constant
realization of what Jane Austen described (in *Emma*) as 'little
zigzags of embarrassment'.

Spanking the Monkey tells the story of a pre-medical student,
Ray (Jeremy Davies), who has completed his first year of college
and stops home in suburban New York on his way to a prestigious
summer internship in Washington D. C. But he finds himself
stranded with his mother (Alberta Watson), who has broken her
leg, while his video-salesman father (Benjamin Hendrickson), too
mean to pay for a nurse, goes on the road. Ray's lot is hard: the
depressed invalid mother – a still attractive woman neglected by
her husband – is demanding; the father's large, beloved dog must
be walked frequently and has a habit of interrupting Ray when he
repairs to the bathroom to jerk off (the film's title is a frat-house
euphemism for masturbation). In an atmosphere of wholesale
embitterment, as if in Oedipal detestation of the obnoxious
absentee husband/father, an intimacy develops between mother
and son and, one sultry night, they make ruinous love. You sense
a cycle of abuse is being perpetuated; Ray tries to kill himself, but
fails.

Spanking the Monkey is clogged, oppressive and very funny. It's also unapologetically real in its depiction of the incestuous collusion between Ray and his mom. It says much of Russell's assurance that he didn't flinch in the face of such unappetizing material, but made it the subject of liberating gallows humor and intense psychological inquiry.

His next film was necessarily lighter. *Flirting with Disaster* is a comparatively zany – but, at heart, equally neurotic – road movie that offers up a satirical overview of 90s America. Mel (Ben Stiller) and Nancy (Patricia Arquette) are a pair of married New York entymologists – new parents, their sex life has gone cold – who embark on a trip to find Mel's birth mother, with an arch, newly divorced adoption agency psychologist, Tina (Tea Leoni), in tow. As they traipse across the country, they encounter a cross-section of Americans, ranging from self-satisfied New Yorkers (Ben's adoptive parents), ageing hippies, bikers, Republicans, and New Agers, to a pair of gay FBI men. All of them give the impression they have seen the light and have adopted a lifestyle to match, but the truth is that none of them – not even older characters, like Ben's two sets of parents – have really grown up and become responsible adults. But Ben has a chance to test his moral fiber when Tina throws herself at him, and Nancy hers when one of the apparently bisexual FBI men tries to seduce her.

Russell has great fun with this gallery of maladjusted archetypes and anti-types, and the movie has the zest of a screwball comedy by Sturges, Capra or Hawks. Underpinning its comedy, though, is the unsentimental recognition that everyone in the movie, and perhaps everyone else everywhere else, is ultimately fucked up. Significantly, *Flirting* is no acme of three-act-structure storytelling; Russell leaves much of the story unresolved, like life itself.

After I'd interviewed Russell for this book of his screenplays, I turned the tape recorder off, and then decided there was one more question that needed to be asked. Was the initial 'O' in his name an homage to David O. Selznick? It wasn't, he said, 'And if it was, I could hardly make the kind of films I want to make.' He's right, of course, but, in a very different way, David O. Russell is as much an iconoclastic independent as the other David O., and one whose eccentric Freudian films may yet prove as treasurable as *Rebecca* and *Duel in the Sun*.

Graham Fuller, June 1996

GRAHAM FULLER: *Were there any aspects of your childhood or teen years that indicated, in retrospect, that you would go on to be a film-maker?*
DAVID O. RUSSELL: I fooled around with an 8mm camera on my block when I was a kid. I wrote a lot of fiction from the age of ten, and thought I would grow up to be a full-time writer. My father was in the sales side of publishing – he eventually became a vice president in sales at Simon & Schuster – so books were revered in our house.

The thing that indicated I might become a director was that I was something of a young impresario. I organized a rock band on my block when I was eight, and I started an alternative newspaper in high school because I had been shut out as an editor by the mainstream paper. I was a bit of a ringleader. Another requirement of being a director is having a rich fantasy life – and I had one. That derived from being isolated out in the suburbs when I was growing up. I remember a lot of long afternoons spent by myself, and also a certain loneliness within my family. I filled it in with a sort of dreaming.

I also watched a lot of TV and movies. Some of the first films I saw were *The Music Man* and *Great Expectations*, which kind of freaked me out, and, of course, *The Wizard of Oz.* My high-school girlfriend, whose grandmother had once owned a United Artists theater, had a card that would get us into any UA theater with as many people as we wanted for free, as many times as we wanted, which, when you're fifteen and broke, is pretty good. So we saw *Shampoo* five times, we saw *All the President's Men, Chinatown* and *Dog Day Afternoon,* all these morally complicated stories. I guess I now attribute to Vietnam and Watergate the fact that all these 70s films were so smart and subversive; people had an appetite for that at the time.

Where did you go to college?
I went to Amherst College. I studied literature and political science; I was always more of a journalist or fiction-writer type than a theater or film type.

What were your literary influences?
In high school J. D. Salinger was a big influence on me, and John Steinbeck – nothing really wild. In college the satirists: Thomas Pynchon, Evelyn Waugh and Mark Twain. I studied fiction-

writing with Henry Bromell, who became a screenwriter, and Mary Gordon, the novelist.

After college, I got sidetracked by radical political work. I worked in Nicaragua for a while, doing literacy work, and taught English as a second language in the South End of Boston. I also worked on improving low-income housing in Lewiston, a mill town in Maine. I vanished into this world for four or five years. I had the idea that I could write at the same time, but I think your hormones get eaten up doing one thing – and mine were getting eaten up living on no money and getting to know a whole new class of people. My parents had been the first people in our family to become middle or upper-middle class, and they hated the fact that I'd gone back to their parents' class – working class; they thought I was throwing my education away. But being a community organizer – getting a whole bunch of people to follow you and say, 'We can improve this housing project, we can clean up this toxic waste dump', and figuring out ways to do it for no money – is quite similar to being an independent film-maker. In fact, I started using video to document housing conditions and I made a documentary about Central American immigrants in Boston. That was my first film. It won a prize and was broadcast on cable networks throughout New England.

And you were continuing to write fiction?
Yes, and some journalism. I wrote for *Jazz Times* and for *In These Times*, a Socialist news magazine.

At what point did you start writing scripts?
Well, I got burned out doing political work, and I decided to go into film-making. This was around the time that Jim Jarmusch and Spike Lee were just getting started, so independent film-making hadn't really caught fire yet. I was slow getting started myself. I took a job working for a PBS documentary series called *Smithsonian World* in Washington, D. C., and I learned a lot about film-making there. One of my jobs was to pick up crews at the airport. They'd fly in from New York and I'd drive them around. They'd tell me they had worked on short films for free, and this was a revelation to me, because I was mystified as to how you put a crew together. Now everybody and their brother does it, but at the time it seemed really difficult.

I moved to New York and took a series of jobs. I worked at a fancy catering company when the late 80s were raging – I was a waiter and bartender at parties at Jacqueline Onassis's and Donald Trump's houses – and as a script-reader for MGM and Punch, Dustin Hoffman's company. Meanwhile I made two short films. The first one, *Bingo Inferno*, was accepted for the Sundance Film Festival [in 1987] and got me a grant from the New York State Council on the Arts to make the second one, *Hairway to the Stars* [1990]. I'm not sure I think either is very good, because I hadn't really found my focus or my style yet.

I then got an NEA [National Endowment of the Arts] grant and another New York State grant for $20,000 apiece to make another short. But I decided at that point that it was time to make a feature. I was on jury duty from my day job writing about the book business for the American Booksellers' Association. I was forced to sit in the jury room and I was in a horrible mood because I had just broken up with a long-term girlfriend, but it was a very productive time because it forced me to write. I knew I wanted to do something different from the clever kind of independent films that were being made, which can often be superficial and trite, and I thought about how Gus Van Sant had made *Mala Noche*. I thought, 'What a ballsy thing: to make a film about a guy's lust for this kid. How can I reach into myself like that and find something revealing or embarrassing, charged in that way, something that would be scary for me to go into, but which I could take other people to?' I wanted to make a film that hadn't been made before, and so I came up with *Spanking the Monkey*. When I wrote it, I went back to the setting and to the idea of sexual discovery that was in my best fiction, the fiction I'd written as an adolescent.

Is Spanking the Monkey *strongly autobiographical?*
It is to the extent that it shows the whole setting of my childhood, of my teenage years and my early college years, when I experienced a breakdown in my family and tried to be a dutiful son when my mother was unhappy and depressed and alone one particular summer. It's a strange configuration. My father traveled a lot, as did a lot of my friends' fathers. When that happens, it's not uncommon for a son to become like a surrogate husband for

his mother. I thought, 'God, what a disgusting, mama's boy, bitch-boy thing to reveal.' And so I decided to go into it.

Can you describe your writing process?
The way I write is, I outline. That's where all the writing happens, then the execution is an embellishment of that. I wrote *Spanking* that way over a period of eighteen months, and I got a lot of feedback, which helped me strengthen it in terms of the structure and how satisfying the overall experience would be. I don't believe you should just say, 'I'm an artist and structure be damned.' I believe in scrutiny and listening to what people have to say, especially since I'd never made a movie before. I had written three or four bad screenplays before I wrote *Spanking*, including a horror script which I did with a friend and had tried to sell. *Spanking* was a departure for me. It was richer and better from the beginning.

How many drafts of it did you write?
It went through ten drafts in those eighteen months. People read it and said, 'Wow, this is very disturbing.' Nobody in Hollywood wanted to make it, but they certainly thought it was powerful and unusual. It kickstarted my career. It got me an agent and a writing assignment at Paramount, through Dolly Parton's company, Sandollar. It was a true story they'd already bought about a high school in Florida that would have been like *Dazed and Confused*, only darker. I knew it wasn't going to work out, but I got paid. Meanwhile, I was trying to get *Spanking* financed. You can spend your whole life doing that. Faye Dunaway liked the script, and I went to her house, which was very exciting because I'd never met a movie star before. We talked about it for a long time, but she had a son of twelve, whom she was raising herself, and she felt squeamish about the material and the effect that it might have on their relationship. I was pulling out all the stops and tried to convince her that it would be good for her relationship with her son and would make him more self-aware. But it didn't work.

How did you finally get the money to make it?
My wife, Janet (who was then my girlfriend), was working at New Line Cinema at the time, so she showed it around, and I had an agent and a couple of producers who shopped it around, too –

everywhere, to all the usual suspects of low-finance movie-making. Nobody wanted to do it. But I met Dean Silvers, an attorney who'd produced a couple of independent films, and he agreed to come on as producer. I had the $40,000 from the two grants. We raised another $40,000 from friends – $1,500 here and there. So we started production with $80,000. Everybody's salaries were deferred. We were also given a lot of 35mm stock and $10,000 worth of motel rooms that we'd bartered for an industrial video. As soon as I finished shooting *Spanking*, I had to go back and shoot a promotional video about this motel complex.

How did you conceive Spanking *visually?*
It was very straightforward, very natural. We wanted it to feel a little documentary-like, not stylized. Very much like a lot of those 70s movies, actually. The style does not call attention to itself, does not say, 'Look at me, I'm a style!' It was a question of using an inconspicuous style that served the purpose of absorbing people in the experience, so that they are drawn in before they realize it, and once they're in, they're uncomfortable, whether they like it or not.

In terms of composition, was there a specific dynamic that you were looking for, particularly in the relationship between Ray and his mom?
We tried to make it feel as claustrophobic as possible, so that you would feel kind of smothered by the mother. You would feel her size; her presence would be larger than Ray's for a lot of the film. For example, we get his perspective when he's putting the cream on her thighs and under her calves. You feel like you're right in there, and it's like her warm breath is on you. Then Ray had this little circuit he was running, like a figure-eight: kitchen, bedroom, bathroom, his mom's room, kitchen, and so on. We get lulled into that maze. It's comforting, but it's awfully suffocating.

You used a lot of disorienting wide angles. I'm thinking of the shot when they're lying on the bed together watching TV.
Yeah, a lot of big masters. Then we get in closer for some grotesque close-ups. I looked at Polanski's *Repulsion* to get that same feeling of Catherine Deneuve being trapped in that house. As a result, details became crucial and I used a lot of cutaways: the close-up on the glass when Ray's mixing his mother a drink; the

clutter on the end-table in the bedroom; stuff on Ray's desk when he's studying. They called me 'The Inserter', as a joke, because we shot all those inserts. It gives you a much richer world and more for your money, especially when you haven't got much.

You also slip extra information into master shots when, for example, Ray's father is in his motel room and we catch a glimpse of a prostitute or his mistress in the background.

Some people think it's a prostitute; to me it was supposed to be 'Betty from Accounting', whom he sees every year; it works either way. I like that throwaway style; I use it in *Flirting With Disaster*, too. It's almost like you're glimpsing things as you're going by, so, as a viewer, you don't feel like you're being shoved into it. It feels like you're being brought into a very real world as a voyeur, where you're suddenly spying on things that happen to clip by the frame. I prefer that kind of style. I also like asymmetrical frames where you don't always see who's talking, or people are framed or cut off in a weird way. I like breaking up the frame by having people walking in and out of it while they're talking.

This seems crucial to your work on a thematic level, because there's an off-centeredness to it. Things come out of the blue visually and narratively. There's also an unsettling sense, in both Spanking the Monkey *and* Flirting With Disaster, *of incompleteness, of something being wrong with the mood. It's like that mood one has some days when you know something's not right with your world, but you can't figure out what it is, then eventually it clicks.*

You know, you get so many different reactions. Some people would watch *Spanking* and deny that there's sexual tension between Ray and his mom. Even though he's showering her and he's dressing her and he's rubbing cream on her, people's power of denial is so great they would just say, 'Well, it's his mom; he's just helping her out,' then they'd be *shocked* to see where the film is going. To me, it's obvious what's going on between them from the beginning.

Did you consciously think about Spanking the Monkey *as a playing out of the Oedipus complex – I mean specifically in psychoanalytic terms?*

I'm very psychologically minded in my own life, so, yes, I did think about that – but that doesn't really take you very far. You wouldn't want just to play the Oedipus complex like a record. To me what is interesting about this family is that it seems almost like there's a collusion between the mother and the father. It was as if the father was saying to the mother, without actually saying or thinking it, 'I'm going away and you're going to be lonely, and Ray'll be in charge of you, so he'll be my substitute, but we're going to pretend like it's not really happening.' I had experienced that and I saw a lot of it in the town where I grew up. So in that sense, it's not just the classic antagonism of the father defending his place against his son. It's more like the father is relinquishing his place to his son.

There's also that Mrs Robinson attitude where the mother's unrealized dream to become a doctor is, in a sense, being fulfilled by the son as he tries to start the career she never had. Yet at the same time she doesn't want him to leave. Once he leaves, it's his own life he's leading, not hers. She can no longer enjoy it vicariously.

Why did you choose medicine as Ray's vocation?
That was a big thing when I was growing up. I was good in science, and that was clearly valued in the suburb of New York where I lived. To become a doctor was the most socially approved thing you could possibly do. It's a care-taking profession, and it's easy for parents to get kudos through a son choosing it as a career.

Tell me about working specifically with Jeremy Davies and Alberta Watson. Did you have a long rehearsal period?
Yes. We had five weeks of rehearsal here in this apartment. I always like long rehearsal periods. I can't imagine walking on a set without having had one. In rehearsal you figure out everything that works and doesn't work, and you also get great new ideas.

How deep into their roles did Alberta and Jeremy go? Was there sexual tension between them, and if so, did you play off it?
I don't think Jeremy ever actually developed a crush or fixation on Alberta, the way I might have in his situation. But it was *very* uncomfortable, because I'd be sitting here saying, 'You're the mother and you're the son. Now, you put your hand here. Now,

you kiss him.' What the rehearsal process weeded out was how explicit we wanted the film to be, and the balance of who was perpetrating what against whom. The mother is not expressly the only perpetrator – Ray is her co-conspirator in a way. In determining how far we could go to make this relationship believable, sustaining that delicate balance was crucial. The single thing I'm most proud of in *Spanking the Monkey* is that it realizes this incestuous relationship *credibly*. You don't look at it and say, 'I don't buy that.' Step by step, there are little signs that it *is* happening. That's what we had to create. I literally had to choreograph it move-by-move, because at what point do you put your hand on your mother's leg? At what point do you do it again, and go further, and how do you go far enough so it's sexual, yet not so far that it's really obvious and she's going to stop you? As a director, you have to say, 'She would stop him at this point.' This was the kind of debate we were constantly having. 'I wouldn't do that,' Jeremy would say. We had to work hard at it to keep it real.

When it came to shooting, did the actors get some kind of release because rehearsal had been so tense?
No. It was an uncomfortable movie to shoot, which is why I subsequently made *Flirting With Disaster* a very light comedy. We only had four weeks to shoot *Spanking* and the mood on the set was uptight because it was an unpleasant thing to live with every day. It was that mood you described, where you sense things aren't quite right, combined with this sexual situation that repulses everybody – or titillates them in a way that is repulsive. People blew up at certain points.

Did that serve the tension in the film?
Absolutely. It was palpable. We had a lot of arguments about how certain scenes would happen, and there were times when Alberta or Jeremy said, 'I won't do this.' For example, the scene in which Ray throws his mother down on the bed and fondles her breasts, well there were versions of that where he actually rapes her, and Jeremy didn't want to do that. I wanted to shoot it three ways. I wanted to shoot one take where he kind of didn't do anything, another where he kind of roughed her up, and one where he went all the way. I got him to do the first two, but not the third.

xvi

We don't actually see them having sex, although it's fully implied that they do.
If I could do it again, I would show more. At the time, I was new to film-making. The closer I got to executing this, the more mortified I was getting. I started to feel, 'This is going to be really gross, and nobody is going to want to see it.' There are people who argue with me that I didn't have to show more, but I'm not convinced. You never stop making a film in your head. You just stop because you have to.

You don't moralize in the film, except in the case of Ray's father, who's a pretty reprehensible character.
I would do that differently also.

The mother appears in a much more human light. You don't come out of the theater hating her despite the fact that she sleeps with her son.
That was very important to me and to Alberta. We didn't want to make her a monster, because then it's just a monster movie. The more you sympathize with her, the more complicated it is, which is why I wish I'd portrayed the father more sympathetically, too.

The film ends with Ray jumping off a cliff, and then hitching a ride with a truck driver. It's a much more ambivalent ending than showing him driving off to college would have been. Also, less glib.
He survives, but you don't know what's going to happen to him or how much damage has been done to him.

How did you go about completing the film in post-production?
As soon as we finished production, we were able to raise roughly another $100,000 for post – on the strength of the rushes. Then we took the film to the 1994 Sundance Film Festival. I was happy it was there but I didn't know how it was going to be received. I was surprised by how well the comedy played and it was amazing to me that it won the Sundance Audience Award. I then made a distribution deal with Fine Line, which had passed on it originally, and we were able to pay everybody who'd worked on a deferred salary. The final cost of the film was about $400,000.

When did you start writing Flirting with Disaster?
As soon as I came back from Sundance. My wife and I talked about it. She said, 'You'd better seize this window of opportunity

before it passes, or you'll have to get a *job*.' I wrote furiously. My son was born around that time, so it was a very chaotic period, which fed into what I was writing. I was a new father, like Mel [Ben Stiller] in the film, my sex life had been disrupted, and I was kind of scared about the commitment and the responsibility. I would never again want to write anything that mirrored my life closely in that way. It's very uncomfortable. You don't have the distance.

Flirting *is another film about the quest for mother, in a way, isn't it?*
Well, after *Spanking the Monkey*, it seemed like a natural step for me to do a comedy about family, to show myself and audiences that I can have a sense of humor about this stuff, that I'm not lugubrious about it. I wrote *Flirting* as a naturalistic, middle-class, almost Woody Allen kind of comedy. It's not grungy, it's not dangerous, it doesn't take place in any kind of cool universe with goatees and syringes and guns.

Why did you choose the road movie format?
After being stuck in this one house in suburban New York for my first movie, it was fun to blow out onto the road and look at a whole bunch of different places. It's great for comedy when the whole country is your palette. You can click into the culture of Southern California Republicans, of the unemployed truckers of the Michigan Rust Belt, of New Mexico desert artists, and then of New York neurotics.

How did it affect your visual style?
I wanted to go for a loose, kinetic quasi-documentary style. That's why I hired [cinematographer] Eric Edwards, because I thought he'd got a very natural look when he shot *My Own Private Idaho* for Gus Van Sant. It was a style that wasn't so bouncy that it called attention to itself, the way that hand-held camera can be. I like that feeling of stalking people on a mission across country that you get on the TV show *Cops*. And when you have eight people in a room or eight people outside and mostly you're shooting them talking, I believe it looks much more interesting and alive if the camera has a natural, rough movement to it.
   My goal was to create very realistic feelings between the characters in *Flirting*. I wanted their interactions to seem authentic

even though farcical things were happening to them. It's high comedy in a very naturalistic setting.

It's a much brighter film than Spanking the Monkey. *You use a very bold, colorful color scheme.*
Well, it's a much happier film. If anything, I started to freak out that it was *too* light. I had set out to make a light comedy and afterward I was bemoaning it. But my wife left a book on the table for me at home. It was a history of screwball comedy. I had never really studied those films, but when I read the book I realized I'd made *Flirting* as a screwball comedy.

It has a Preston Sturges quality to it. I'm surprised to find he wasn't a specific influence on you.
I looked at Sturges' *The Lady Eve* recently and I liked it a lot, but he hadn't influenced me. I was more influenced by films like *Shampoo* and *The Heartbreak Kid*, these realistic-feeling, neurotic 70s comedies, in which people are very deadpan and it takes a while for the jokes to unfold. *Flirting*'s not really about jokes or snappy dialogue, though. It's about people's behavior in ridiculous situations and how they respond if something weird or horrible ambushes them. I'm interested in the juxtaposition of outrageous events with so-called 'normal' behavior. In life, outrageous things happen to us all the time, many of them consciously or unconsciously instigated by ourselves. Our unexpressed desires can't help coming out and making messy, complicated situations that we then try to play down. We're always trying to cover our tracks.

Did you see the film primarily through Mel's eyes?
Yes. He's kind of like the Stealth bomber who's trying to fly under the radar.

You mean in his hovering around Tina [Téa Leoni] – the disaster he's flirting with?
Yes. He's not sure he really wants to do it and then get booted out of his marriage by Nancy [Patricia Arquette]. He's trying to see how far he can go without committing himself, and he's also trying to be the nice-guy husband to his wife while pursuing these more unpleasant desires and rebellions.

You keep throwing in surprise characters throughout the movie.
Surprise, for me, is the *m.o.* of this comedy. I didn't want people
to be able to predict where it was going or where the humor was
coming from, and I feel I achieved that. The idea was to ambush
the viewer.

*Where did the gay FBI men, Paul [Richard Jenkins] and Tony [Josh
Brolin], come from?*
I had been reading about Clyde Tolson and J. Edgar Hoover, and
I wanted to have a relationship like that in the film. But I wanted
to do it in a very straight, not fruity way. I know a lot of gay men
who are regular guys. I like the counterpoint of these macho G-
men being homosexuals.

I also wanted to show a cross-section of different kinds of
couples in the film, to show that certain issues are universal. Gay
or straight, old or young – many couples fall into the same
patterns of behaviour, which I find very interesting. One person in
a relationship may be more controlling and one person more of a
wanderer. One person may be more grounded and one person
more flighty. Couples can have a hard time keeping their intimacy
alive and I liked showing that it can happen across the board.

*You were working with stars for the first time, and with bigger groups of
actors. How did that experience compare with the experience you had on*
Spanking the Monkey?
It was completely different and totally educational. It's hard to
imagine that any other film would feel as pressured to me as
Flirting, because I was dealing with so many firsts. It was my first
time with a real budget, the first time that I was being paid, the
first time that I was dealing with celebrities, and the first time that
I was dealing with a story that has the kind of humor that needs to
be effervescent yet grounded. That's a real tough thing to sustain –
the hardest thing of all.

Also having so many people in every scene made it very difficult
to keep each scene alive, which to me is the first order of business.
Practically every scene in *Flirting* has five to eight principals in it,
which is a headache for coverage and the eyeline – it's one I
wouldn't want to have again any time soon.

How did you solve the problem?
We rehearsed a lot, as on *Spanking*, and I rewrote much of the
script in rehearsal, because the actors were bringing in very useful
things that meant we could lose other things. We also tried to
figure out how to block a scene in a way that was kinetic. With
eight people in a scene, it's hard to keep everybody present. It's
easy for certain people to disappear, or you can end up playing to
three or four of them. Also, Eric videotaped our rehearsals and we
studied the tapes.

*It's said that an artist really needs just one idea. You seem to have
tapped a vein of neurotic family comedy and made it uniquely yours.*
But I'm off that now. I'm tired of it. It was OK for two movies,
and maybe I'll come back to it later, but I want to depart into
bigger worlds that give me more metaphoric license. *Spanking* and
Flirting were fun films to make, but they were very restrictive in
the sense that I was tied to a certain level of reality. I didn't have a
lot of poetic license to talk about the bigger political and religious
issues that interest me. My next film is a period thriller in the vein
of *Chinatown*, but set in an earlier period.

*Given your social concerns, why didn't you start out with a political or
message film?*
I was really learning how to make a movie and how to deal with
in-depth characters. I'm still learning, but I feel confident about
that now and ready to move into a world that deals with social
questions. *Flirting* actually had a little more of a patina of politics
than *Spanking*. You've got the Reaganite woman [Celia Weston]
who shows up, you've got little snips and bites of politics here and
there.

And you now plan to alternate between comedies and serious films?
Yes. It's refreshing. When you make a film, you live in the same
energy for two years. To live in comedic energy again for two years
would, I think, tire me out. I feel like making something dark now.

Flirting with Disaster

CREDITS

MEL	Ben Stiller
NANCY	Patricia Arquette
TINA	Tea Leoni
PEARL COPLIN	Mary Tyler Moore
EDDIE COPLIN	George Segal
RICHARD SCHLICHTING	Alan Alda
MARY SCHLICHTING	Lily Tomlin
PAUL	Richard Jenkins
TONY	Josh Brolin
VALERIE SWANEY	Celia Weston
LONNIE	Glenn Fitzgerald
JANE	Beth Ostrosky
SANDRA	Cynthia Lamontage
FRITZ BOUDREAU	David Patrick Kelly
MITCH	John Ford Noonan
B AND B LADY	Charlet Oberly
JILL	Nadia Dajani

CREW

Written and Directed by	David O. Russell
Produced by	Dean Silvers
Casting by	Ellen Parks
	Risa Bramon Garcia
Music Supervisor	Bonnie Greenberg
Costume Designer	Ellen Lutter
Production Designer	Kevin Thompson
Editor	Christopher Tellefsen
Director of Photography	Eric Edwards
Associate Producer	Christopher Goode
Co-Producer	Kerry Orent
Co-Executive Producer	Trea Hoving
Executive Producer	Bob Weinstein
	Harvey Weinstein

EXT. CITY STREET – NEW YORK CITY – DAY

A RICH, SMART WOMAN *walks by.*

> *[MEL
> (voice-over)

My mother could be rich. She could be rich and smart. Or she could be rich and stupid.

A RICH, STUPID WOMAN *walks by.*

On the other hand, she could be poor and good-hearted.

A WIDOW *carrying flowers and rosary beads walks toward the
camera.*

Or she could be poor and mean.

A TOUGH WOMAN *approaches a parked car and smashes the driver's
window.*
CUT TO:]

INT. ADOPTION OFFICE – NEW YORK CITY – DAY

MEL *sits in a cluttered office opposite an* ADOPTION COUNSELOR *at her
cluttered desk.*

> MEL

I mean, I have no idea what she's like.
CUT TO:

EXT. CITY STREET – NEW YORK CITY – DAY

> MEL

Then there's my father, right?

A series of DIFFERENT MEN *walk toward the camera,* JUMP CUT
one after the other.

*Added during filming

3

I look at guys on the street every day – regular guys, walking down the street. And depending on my mood, I imagine that any one of them could be my father. This guy. How about this guy . . .

A BARE-CHESTED MAN *rifles through a garbage can and gives the finger to passersby.*

'Hi Dad!.' Then I have to picture these two people having sex.

Now a series of DIFFERENT COUPLES *walk toward the camera, one pair after the other. Mix and match the* RICH, SMART WOMAN *with the* BARE-CHESTED MAN, *the* POOR, GOOD-HEARTED WOMAN *with the* CARPET SALESMAN, *etc.*

Okay, maybe they're not together now, but at least thirty years ago they had to hook up in order to have me, right? Mix and match, mix and match, all these people together.

Cut from one PROSPECTIVE MOTHER *to another, standing before the camera.*

I can't help feeling, that if I'd been raised by at least one of my real parents, I wouldn't be such a nervous person, you know? I might be living a completely different life, in a totally different city.

Cut from one PROSPECTIVE WIFE *to another, walking toward the camera.*

I could be married to a totally different person with a different job. I mean, how do I know? I don't. Anything's possible.

CUT TO:

INT. ADOPTION OFFICE – NEW YORK CITY – DAY

MEL *sits talking to the* WOMAN, *behind a desk:* TINA KALB. *We hear the clicking of a computer.*

TINA
(*off screen*)

Well, the mystery of your unknown self is about to unfold. Your mother lives in San Diego, California.

More typing.

Her name is Valerie Swaney.

6

                          MEL

Valerie Swaney?

                          TINA
                       (*off screen*)
I told you it wouldn't take long.

                          MEL

Can we arrange a meeting . . . soon?

                          TINA
                       (*off screen*)
How's next month?

                          MEL

No, no, I told Nancy I'd do it sooner. I've been driving her crazy.

                          TINA
                       (*off screen*)
Because you can't name your son?

                          MEL

I've just been distracted and tense ever since the baby was born.

                          TINA
                       (*off screen*)
A little unsteady?

                          MEL

Preoccupied.

   CUT TO: *Opening credit sequence* INTERCUT *with* –

INT. MEL AND NANCY'S BEDROOM – NEW YORK CITY – DAY

A thirty-year-old attractive WOMAN *comes in wearing a kimono and a
shower cap. She takes the robe off with her back to the camera. She is
wearing nothing under the robe. She opens a drawer and takes out a
piece of lingerie, a teddy. She puts it on with her back to the camera and
looks at herself in a full-length mirror. She self-consciously holds her
tummy in to flatten it. She goes back to the drawer. Takes out a loose,
flowing, short nightie. With her back to the camera, she takes off the
teddy and puts on the nightie. She is happier with this loose-fitting
garment.*

                           7

She now arranges herself attractively on the bed, lying back on a pillow. And waits. After a moment, she changes to a different position. And waits. She looks at her watch. Then she takes her watch off and puts it on the night table. She gets up, takes off her shower cap, fixes her hair in the mirror. Returns to the bed. Lies down seductively. Waits. Picks up a book, starts reading.

Now we hear the front door of the apartment open and close. We hear a man's voice call to her from inside the apartment.

MEL
(calls off screen)

Nancy?

NANCY
(calls back)

I'm in the bedroom.

She positions herself deliciously on the bed. MEL *comes in, he looks harried. He wears a sports coat, a tie, a white shirt, glasses.*

MEL

Have I got some big news.

He proceeds to face the bureau and take his tie off.

You look great. Why are you dressed like that?

NANCY

Did you forget about our date?

MEL

Oh, my God, I'm sorry.

NANCY

You're here now, that's what counts.

She kneels on the bed and holds her arms open to him. He walks over and she holds him.

MEL

I feel so bad.

NANCY

That's all right, we planned this, we're not going to fight.

MEL

I want you to know why I forgot –

NANCY

Shhh-shh.

She kisses him deeply. He caresses her, finds her breasts in his hands, grows aroused. They talk as they make out and caress.

MEL

You look very sexy.

NANCY

I feel fat.

MEL

Give yourself a break, you're getting there.

NANCY
(*opening his pants*)

What does that mean, I'm getting there?

MEL

It means you look sexy.

9

He starts nuzzling and kissing her neck as she kneels on the bed.

NANCY

Take your shoes off.

MEL

We've got to talk –

NANCY

No talking.

She starts to go down on him. He curls around in order to go down on her. In turn, she pulls away to go down on him, and he pulls away to go down on her. Finally, she stops and sits up.

You never let me do this anymore.

MEL

Are we going to fight over who's going down on who?

NANCY

No, because you said you're going to try to relax. Now come on, honey.

MEL

I can't sit back like that, it makes me uncomfortable.

NANCY
(*tickling him*)
You can't let go of any control, can you? Can you?

MEL

Don't do that. Stop it.

He is squirming away from her across the bed.

The tickling stops and she starts kissing him deeply and it is very arousing. She's opened him up and relaxed him.

The BABY starts crying faintly down the hall. They continue to kiss for a moment, then they both look anxiously over their shoulders. She stands up.

NANCY

Nap time's over.

MEL *jumps up.*

MEL

I'll get him.

He starts to put his pants on.

NANCY

You don't have to put your pants on to get the baby.

MEL

Okay.

He tosses them down.

INT. HALLWAY – DAY

MEL *rushes down the hall, into the bathroom.*

INT. BATHROOM – DAY

He fishes in the hamper and pulls out a pair of dirty jeans and puts them on.
  CUT TO:

INT. HALLWAY – DAY

MEL *walks into the nursery.*

He emerges kissing and comforting the crying BABY *and continues to the living room.*

MEL

Shhh, it's OK, it's OK.

INT. LIVING ROOM – DAY

A very attractive professional woman wearing a suit and flats sits on the edge of the couch waiting. This is TINA KALB.

MEL *rushes in carrying the crying baby. She looks at his one shoe, his disheveled hair, half-unbuttoned shirt.*

TINA

I feel like I'm keeping you from something.

11

                              MEL

No, no, this is a priority.

                              TINA

Is it a bad time for your wife?

                              MEL

It's fine, we just need another few minutes. Can I get you
something to drink?

                              TINA

I'd love a glass of water.

   MEL *rushes into the kitchen.*

INT. KITCHEN – DAY

He gets a glass of water.
   CUT TO:

INT. HALLWAY – DAY

MEL *rushes down the hall with the* BABY *and the glass of water, almost
goes into the bedroom, stops short, goes back to the living room, and
gives* TINA *the glass of water.*

                              TINA

Thanks.
   CUT TO:

INT. HALLWAY – DAY

MEL *rushes down the hall with the* BABY, *stops, backs up, goes into the
bathroom and takes the jeans off.*
   CUT TO:

INT. BEDROOM – DAY

MEL *comes in with the* BABY *and sits on the bed. He is starting to look
fairly frazzled.*

                         [*NANCY

I love the way he looks around.

*Cut from completed film

                              12

MEL

He's making sure the world didn't disappear while he was
sleeping. Here you go –]

He tries to hand her the BABY.

NANCY

No, this is good, he'll keep your hands occupied.

MEL

We can make another date, honey, come on.

*She pulls him reluctantly toward her with one hand and kisses him
passionately. She kisses his neck, then starts to go down on him while
he holds the* BABY. MEL *sits holding the* BABY *at arm's length. The*
BABY *is looking straight at him.*

Nancy. I can't do this.

She continues to blow him.

His little eyes are looking at me. Nancy?

She continues.

My real mother lives in San Diego.

Pause. She sits up and looks confused.

NANCY

What?

MEL

That's what I wanted to tell you. I went to the adoption agency
and they found my real mother.

NANCY

You just walked in and they found your mother?

MEL

It was the second meeting, actually.

NANCY

Wow. Why didn't we think about it before?

                              MEL
I don't know. I was avoiding it.

                            NANCY
This will help you name the baby.

                              MEL
Absolutely.

                            NANCY
I'm so happy about this.

   She hugs him and kisses him.

                              MEL
Why don't you put something on and come out and meet Tina?

                            NANCY
Who?

                              MEL
The woman from the agency.

                            NANCY
This woman is here in our apartment?

                              MEL
I tried to explain but you're all sexed up.

                            NANCY
I'm sexed up because we had a date, not because I'm some kind of
a freak –

                              MEL
I know you're not a freak, it was a simple misunderstanding, OK?

                            NANCY
Now I feel stupid.

                              MEL
Hey, this is a good thing, isn't it?

                            NANCY
Yeah.

MEL

OK, come on.

He kisses her on top of her head.
CUT TO:

INT. LIVING ROOM – DAY

NANCY *walks in barefoot, wearing her kimono. She sees* MEL *standing with* TINA, *who now holds the* BABY.

TINA

Hi, I'm Tina Kalb –

NANCY *and* TINA *shake hands.*

NANCY

Hi.

TINA

I'm sorry to barge in on you like this, but Mel said he didn't want to waste any time.

MEL

Nancy understands how important this is.

TINA

The baby's gorgeous, by the way. He looks exactly like Mel.

NANCY

Actually, a lot of people say he looks like me.

TINA

What do I know? I'm just another thirty-five-year-old woman desperate for a baby of her own.

NANCY

Doesn't your husband want children?

NANCY *takes the* BABY *from* TINA*'s arms.*

TINA

I'm in the middle of a divorce, actually. I just can't seem to part with the ring.

She pulls it off her finger and puts it into her purse.

NANCY

Oh, I'm sorry.

TINA

It was one of those dead marriages where you have to start making
dates to try to have sex.

MEL *and* NANCY *look at* TINA *uncomfortably.*

MEL

I'm sure you'll get married again.

TINA

At this point it might be easier to just find an intelligent man to
impregnate me.

She bursts out laughing, joined by MEL.

NANCY

Excuse me, but I don't understand exactly who you are.

MEL

Didn't I tell you she's doing the study and everything?

NANCY

No.

TINA

I'm sorry, I'll be going to San Diego next week to document the
reunion. (*hands papers to* NANCY)
Nancy, I have some waivers I need you to get back to me.

NANCY

You want to go next week?

MEL

They're going to pay for everything because of the study, isn't that
great?

TINA

There's a dearth of documentation on the psychic impact these
reunions have on the spouse, for instance you, as well as Mel's
adoptive parents.

                    NANCY

Are you a psychologist?

                    TINA

Not quite, I'm still finishing my doctorate.

                    MEL

She used to be a dancer.

                    TINA

That was a long time ago.
                    (*looks at her watch*)
I need to call the office.

                    NANCY

The phone's in the kitchen.

                    TINA

That's all right, I've got one right here.

TINA *pulls out a portable phone as she steps into the adjoining dining
room.* MEL *absently stares at* TINA *as she stands in the next room
with the phone. Then* MEL *turns back and sees* NANCY *staring at
him; they look at each other awkwardly.*

                    MEL

She's great, isn't she?
    CUT TO:

INT. MUSEUM OF NATURAL HISTORY – DAY

NANCY *and* JILL *work on a stone-age man diorama.*

                    JILL

After I had my baby I wanted my husband to stay home and help
with the night feedings. Not drag me on some plane to San Diego.

                    NANCY

I like traveling. The baby's five months old. I really think this is
going to get us closer together.

                    JILL

Oh honey, after you're married he feels like he's kissing his mother
half the time, anyway.

                    17

NANCY

Our kissing is still nice. But he's so controlling about the oral sex.

JILL

Well have you tried the warm water method?

NANCY

You're kidding.

JILL

No, Joe loves it.

MEL *enters pushing a cart with dead insect boxes. He holds two large dead beetles. He wears a white lab coat.*

NANCY

Hey.

JILL

Oh, hi, Mel.

MEL

Look what I found.

NANCY

What did you find?

MEL *shows them the beetles.*

What made you dig these out?

MEL

I don't know. I was just feeling nostalgic for some reason.

NANCY

That's so sweet. We found these on our first field trip together.

JILL

Very sweet. Oh, congratulations on finding your mother, Mel.

MEL

Thank you.

JILL

That ought to settle some big issues for you, huh?

MEL

Definitely. Which issues are you talking about?

JILL

Starting with the whole sex thing . . .

NANCY

The baby's name. 'Cause you said that 'Ethan' –

MEL

– No, wait a minute. She just said 'the whole sex thing'.

NANCY

– 'Cause you said that 'Ethan' was too feminine.

MEL

Right . . .

NANCY

So we were trying to think of a more masculine baby name, right?

MEL

Okay, but she said the 'sex thing'. Didn't you just say the 'sex thing'?

NANCY

But she meant that.

MEL

Why don't you just let her speak for herself? What did you mean?

JILL

Actually, it was oral sex I was referring to.

MEL

Oh, oral sex. Really? I think I just walked in on a ladies' conversation that guys aren't supposed to hear.

NANCY

No, you didn't.

MEL

Yes, and I'm going to go. I'm going to leave.

NANCY

No stay. Don't go. C'mon.

19

MEL
(*backing out*)

No, leave, go. Stay, no.

NANCY

Honey, we weren't talking about us.

MEL

What?

NANCY

I wouldn't . . . you've got to know that.

MEL

I know that so much. It's so true.
CUT TO:

EXT. NEW YORK CITY – NIGHT

MEL *and* NANCY *walk hand in hand.*

*[MEL

Hey, I didn't go around telling my friends you didn't want to
make love for almost two months after the baby was born, did I?

NANCY

Probably.

MEL

OK, but it didn't get back to you, did it?

NANCY *laughs.*

Are you sure you're okay with this woman coming along? It's not
weird or anything?

NANCY

Well, it's a little strange to be traveling with a chaperone. But if
you're OK with it, I'm OK with it.

MEL

Well, it's just she's been through the process so many times. I
think it's a good thing.

*Added during filming

20

NANCY

Honey, if this helps you get what you need inside, then I'm all for it.]

They kiss.
CUT TO:

INT. MAYFAIR HOTEL BAR – NIGHT

MEL *sits at a banquet, waiting and sipping tea. He looks at his watch.*
TINA *comes sweeping into the room, wearing another smart suit and carrying a wet umbrella.*

*[MEL

Hi.

MEL *stands to greet her. She sits down, taking her jacket off.*

TINA

I'm sorry I'm late, but I had this excruciating meeting with my attorney. If you ever get divorced, don't go the mediation route.

MEL

This is such a gorgeous place you picked.

TINA

Do you like it?

MEL

Very much, I've never been here.

TINA

I always come here when I'm sad and I need to feel part of the world again. So, did you make the date to tell your parents?

MEL

Actually, I need to talk to you about that.

TINA

Why, are you having second thoughts?

An old WAITER hovers over the table.

WAITER

Another herbal tea, sir?

*Cut from completed film

TINA

Herbal tea? It's after five o'clock, isn't it? I'll have a vodka Martini up with a twist.

MEL

I think I'll have a Martini, also.

TINA

Good.

The WAITER *nods and starts to leave.*

MEL

No, I better stick with the tea.

TINA
(*she lights a cigarette, exhales*)
So, your wife just came back from maternity leave and you need to save the vacation time so you can be together, right?

MEL

Actually, that's true, but –

TINA

It's fine with me. I just thought you had a sense of urgency when you first came in. You said you feel like you don't have an anchor, that was your word.

MEL

That's still true.

TINA

And we got the funding and it was a big break for me, which wasn't easy, by the way. I mean, every Tom, Dick, and Harry wants to find his parents these days.

MEL

We were lucky to get that, weren't we?

TINA

Absolutely. And then there's the issue of your son's real lineage.

The WAITER *puts the drinks down.*

MEL

I said I wanted the tea.

WAITER

I'm sorry, I thought you said the Martini.

MEL

Forget it.

WAITER

I can bring you the tea.

TINA

It's OK, forget it.

TINA *looks at* MEL *while she sips her Martini thoughtfully.*

MEL

I don't want to cancel the trip. I just don't want to tell my adoptive parents.

TINA
(*smiles*)
Oh. That's perfectly natural. I'm sorry I over-reacted. Why don't you want to tell them?

MEL

They're very emotional people. They're not going to like it.

TINA

Of course they're not, but that's why you have to do it. I mean, if you want to redefine your family, you've got to –

She rifles through her briefcase for documents. It is a disorganized mess.

MEL

How did you get into this field, anyway?

TINA

I wanted to resolve my own issues with commitment and happiness and all that shit – why does anyone become a shrink?
(*pulls out papers and hands them to him*)
See if these materials don't help. They were written by others in precisely your situation.

23

MEL *puts on his reading glasses and glances down at the materials.*

Those glasses are great, where'd you get them?

MEL

Robert Mark on 71st Street. Nancy thinks they make me look too
cold.

TINA

Not at all, they make you look kind of paternal.

MEL

Thanks.

TINA

Do you like being a father?

MEL

Oh, yeah. It's pretty amazing.

TINA

I hear the sex gets better and better.

MEL
(*stunned*)

What?

TINA

I'm sorry, that's none of my business.

MEL

No, no, that's all right. Who told you that?

TINA

My friend Jackie said she had twice as many orgasms during the
pregnancy and then after the birth, too. Have you found that to be
the case?

MEL

Oh, definitely.

TINA

Good. Good for you.]
CUT TO:

INT. MEL AND NANCY'S LIVING ROOM – DAY

MR COPLIN *is an attractive, sixty-year-old man who sits on the sofa facing a tray of cheese and crackers on the coffee table.* MRS COPLIN *is a trim, attractive sixty-year-old woman who stands next to the table.* MEL *is wearing his glasses.*

MR COPLIN

This cheese is disgusting, get it away from me.

MRS COPLIN

What's wrong with this cheese?

MEL

Listen, I'd like you to meet Tina Kalb, who's here because –

MRS COPLIN *dips a cracker into some cheese and eats it.* NANCY *sits with the* BABY *on her lap while* MEL *stands.*

MR COPLIN

It smells like vomit.

MRS COPLIN

Stop being such a baby.

MR COPLIN

I don't like cheese, so I'm a baby?

NANCY *takes* MEL*'s glasses off his face.*

NANCY

Why are you wearing these?

MRS COPLIN

Did you get the support bra yet?

NANCY

Not yet.

MRS COPLIN

What are you waiting for?

NANCY

Please stop making such a big deal out of it.

MRS COPLIN

It makes a real difference.

MEL

We're not going to talk about this now.

MRS COPLIN

Yes, we are. I want you to look at this.

MRS COPLIN *suddenly yanks her blouse up over her bra. She has a good figure for her age.*

MR COPLIN

For God's sake.

NANCY

Very nice, Pearl.

MRS COPLIN

I want you to consider my age and ask yourself how I maintain this.

MEL

Could you stop this? I want to introduce you to someone –

MRS COPLIN

I couldn't have a baby, but I still had to fight the laws of gravity. You need the help of a good bra, and believe me, if you want to keep your husband's attention, you better get one, pronto.

She drops her shirt and picks up some cheese.

MEL

Thank you very much.

MR COPLIN

I hope you're satisfied.

MRS COPLIN

I'm not doing this for my sake.

NANCY

If my breasts drop, they drop, there's nothing I can do about it.

NANCY *holds a cookie.*

MEL

That's right. Good for you, Nancy. You've had five of those,
honey.

She looks him in the eye and pops it into her mouth.

MR COPLIN

Enough with the breasts, Pearl.

MRS COPLIN *studies* TINA*'s body.*

MRS COPLIN

Your friend's very long-waisted, isn't she?

MEL

OK, that's it. We're not going to talk about this anymore.

MRS COPLIN

It's a free country. Why can't I talk?

MR COPLIN
(*shouts*)

You can't leave well enough alone, can you, Pearl?

MRS COPLIN

Why don't *you* leave me alone?

MRS COPLIN *picks up a piece of cheese and holds it up to* MR
COPLIN*'s face.*

MR COPLIN

Get that the hell away from me before I knock it away.

MRS COPLIN

Oh, you're gonna hit me in front of all these people?

MR COPLIN

Don't tempt me.

MEL
(*shouts*)

Will you stop acting like this?

MRS COPLIN
(*rushes up, whispering*)

Don't yell around the baby.

NANCY

He wouldn't have to yell if you'd listen to him for two seconds.

MR COPLIN

What's gotten into my sweet daughter-in-law all of a sudden?

MRS COPLIN

Hormones, no mystery there.

MEL *runs his hands over his face, trying to calm himself.* MRS COPLIN *takes the* BABY *from* NANCY*'s arms.*

MR COPLIN

Does this baby have a name yet?

TINA

Four months old without a name?

NANCY

Don't blame me. I like Ethan.

MEL

No, Ethan's too lame.

NANCY

He thinks everything's too lame or too bold.

MRS COPLIN

What kind of embarrassing, neurotic thing is this, Mel?

MEL

It's a question of my real background and my real identity.

MR COPLIN

That's ridiculous. You're Mel Coplin, that's who you are.

TINA

This process will go a long way toward clarifying that identity issue.

MRS COPLIN

What process? Who is this new friend with the camera, already?

MEL

I've only been trying to introduce her for the last ten minutes. She's here for a very important reason –

TINA *focuses the camcorder on* MRS COPLIN, *who stares into the lens.*

MRS COPLIN

Oh, my God. You're getting a divorce. She's a counselor. No.
She's a lawyer.

MEL

Will you shut up?

MR COPLIN

Don't talk to your mother like that.

MEL

We're not getting a divorce.

MR COPLIN

Maybe you should, if you can't name your baby.

MRS COPLIN

That is a terrible, sick thing to say, Ed.

MR COPLIN

You said it first.

MRS COPLIN

That's no excuse.

MR COPLIN

If you say it, fine, but if I say it I'm sick.

MEL

Tina works at the adoption agency.

They look at MEL.

MRS COPLIN

Excuse me?

MR COPLIN

What adoption agency?

MEL

The private adoption agency where you got me when I was a little
baby.

MRS COPLIN

Oh, my God.

She sits down, and rifles through her bag for a cigarette.

TINA

Damn it, the camera just jammed. A brand new camera. That was such an important moment.

MRS COPLIN
(*lights up*)

I have to have a cigarette if we're going to talk about this.

TINA

Can I have one of those?

MRS COPLIN *gives* TINA *a cigarette.*

NANCY

Youy can't smoke around the baby.

MRS COPLIN
(*drags deeply on cigarette*)

Show a little compassion.

TINA
(*tinkering with camera*)

This might be a good time to make an exception for her.

NANCY

Please put it out, Pearl.

MRS COPLIN

I'd like to know what happened to the constitution in this country.

She drags, exhales smoke.

NANCY

Pearl.

MRS COPLIN
(*puts cigarette out*)

All right, it's out, OK? Why does he need to do this roots thing? Aren't we good enough parents?

TINA

You did the best you could. Psychic scars can't be helped.

MR COPLIN

Psychic scars? What is she talking about?

Mrs Coplin starts to cry quietly with her face in her hands. Mr Coplin pats her on the back gently to comfort her. They all watch.

MRS COPLIN
(*quietly*)

She's saying we failed completely.

MEL
(*quietly*)

That's way too extreme.

MRS COPLIN
(*crying*)

Yeah. Just maybe forty percent –

MEL
(*quietly*)

You can't quantify it like that. What difference does it make if it's forty percent or sixty percent?

MRS COPLIN

Sixty percent!

MR COPLIN

Why is everyone so serious all of a sudden? I thought we were
going to talk about buying you new carpeting.

MRS COPLIN

Your life is so rich, so full. You've got a wife, a child, a good job,
so why are you doing this now?

MEL

I have to do it. It's my right.

MRS COPLIN

Your right? What does that mean?

TINA

No matter where we are in our lives, particularly if we're adopted,
we can't help feeling there's something we need to find out there
that's going to make us whole, happy, and free.

MR COPLIN

When she puts it like that, it makes me want to do it, too.

MRS COPLIN

This woman strikes me as very dangerous.

TINA

It's understandable you'd find me threatening.

MRS COPLIN

Oh, why don't you psychoanalyze me, go ahead. I'm abrasive,
pushy, defensive, my husband is food-phobic and passive-
aggressive –

MEL

The point is – we're leaving for San Diego in the morning and I
have every intention of –

MRS COPLIN
(*wiping her face*)
What about your father's sixtieth birthday?

MEL

Can I finish my sentence, please? I have every intention of returning for Dad's birthday.

MR COPLIN

You're aware there's a big car theft problem in San Diego.

MEL

No, I didn't know that.

TINA

I haven't heard anything about that.

MR COPLIN

They bump you, and when you stop they mutilate you and take your car.

MRS COPLIN

It happened to Art Sackheim.

NANCY

They killed Art Sackheim?

MR COPLIN

Don't be ridiculous. They bumped him and took his car. Who said anything about killing?

MRS COPLIN
(*wiping her eyes*)

Enjoy yourself. I understand they have a lovely zoo in San Diego.
   CUT TO:

EXT. WEST 83RD STREET MANHATTAN – DAY

MEL *and* NANCY *walk out of their pre-war apartment building.* MEL *carries the suitcases;* NANCY *carries the* BABY *and the car seat.*

They approach the Town Car that is waiting with a DRIVER *and an open trunk, and* TINA *jumps out of the car, wearing a miniskirt and flats, with the camcorder in her hand.*

MEL *is wearing his glasses again.* NANCY *looks* TINA *up and down.*

TINA

All set?

33

MEL

I think so.

> *They get into the car.*
> CUT TO:

INT. RENTAL CAR – SAN DIEGO – DAY

MEL *drives along the freeway in a white rental car past sunny palm trees and bright green lawns with automatic sprinklers.* TINA *sits in the passenger seat.* NANCY *sits in back with the* BABY *in a baby car seat.*

As they drive along the open highway on the outskirts of San Diego, the car passes a sign reading 'John Wayne international airport'.

NANCY
(*squinting*)

It certainly is sunny out here, isn't it?

TINA

Are you nervous?

MEL

No, I feel exhilarated.

> *Suddenly there is a black van tailgating* MEL, *honking loudly and incessantly.*

Oh, my God, it's happening.

NANCY

What's happening?

MEL

The bump and rob.

NANCY

Don't panic.

> *The van pulls alongside* MEL *and a* BLACK GUY *honks the horn and leans out the window.*

BLACK GUY
(*shouts*)

Pull over.

34

TINA

Close the window.

MEL frantically tries to close his window but can't find the button.

MEL

I can't find the switch.

BLACK GUY
(shouts)

Yo. Yo.

MEL
(shouts)

Get away from me.

The BLACK GUY throws a jacket into MEL's window.

BLACK GUY
(shouts)

You left your jacket in the parking lot, man.

MEL
(shouts)

Thank you very much.

CUT TO:

EXT. VALERIE'S HOUSE – SAN DIEGO – DAY

It is a sunny, quiet, upper-middle-class street of good-sized ranch houses in San Diego. MEL wear his glasses and walks from the rental car parked on the street toward a particular ranch house with a Cadillac in the driveway. NANCY walks alongside him carrying the BABY, and TINA follows, taping with the camcorder. They walk up the slate path to the door and stand there. MEL looks nervous. NANCY reaches over and takes his glasses off. They stare at the front door nervously.

NANCY

Should I ring the bell?

MEL

Yes. I mean no, wait.

It's too late. NANCY has rung the bell.

35

I told you to wait.

                    NANCY
You said yes first.

                    MEL
You didn't give me a chance to change my mind.

> *The door opens and a six foot-two-inch woman appears. This is*
> VALERIE, MEL*'s biological mother. She has frosted hair, is about*
> *fifty, and somewhat pretty.*

> *She wears bright orange prints and San Diego colors.*

                    VALERIE
What a pretty wife you have, and I see you brought your nanny.

                    NANCY
I'm not the nanny, I'm the wife.

                    VALERIE
Oh, excuse me. What a terrible way to start.

                    TINA
Tina Kalb from the Maidstone Adoption Agency.

> *She shakes* VALERIE*'s hand.* VALERIE *and* MEL *look at each other.*
> *He nervously shakes* VALERIE*'s hand.*

                    VALERIE
Valerie Swaney.

                    MEL
Mel Coplin.

> *They look at each other awkwardly. Suddenly they embrace each other.*
> *Because she is so tall,* MEL *is hugging her around the waist. He and*
> NANCY *exchange looks while his cheek is buried in* VALERIE*'s chest.*
> CUT TO:

INT. VALERIE'S ENTRY HALL

They walk in. MEL *suddenly notices the Ronald Reagan portrait.*

                    VALERIE
He's a great man.

I always wondered if I should've appreciated him more.

NANCY *looks unabashedly shocked.*
CUT TO:

INT. VALERIE'S DINING ROOM – DAY

A contemporary California room with silvery wallpaper.

VALERIE *sits at the table, dabbing her eyes.* MEL *also looks a little teary.* NANCY *holds the* BABY, *and* TINA *holds the camera on her lap. They do not speak for a moment.*

VALERIE

Your daddy was short.

MEL

That would explain it.

She reaches out and touches MEL*'s forehead.*

VALERIE

We have the same forehead, don't we? And the same eyes.

MEL *studies her forehead and nods.*

MEL

This is amazing. I've never shared physical traits with family before.

He looks at her.

VALERIE

I'm a bad person for what I did to you.

MEL

Don't say that.

VALERIE

It's true.

She puts her hands over her face and starts crying again. MEL *reaches out and holds her wrist; he looks tearful.*

NANCY *and* TINA *watch, teary-eyed.*

37

MEL

Listen to me. Tina says that many mothers who gave their children up for adoption in the sixties were independent young women acting against a conservative world.

VALERIE

You're saying I was a slut.

MEL

No.

VALERIE

Oh, God.

She jumps up and runs to the kitchen.

MEL
(*calls after her*)

You're not a slut.

INT. VALERIE'S KITCHEN – DAY

VALERIE *freshens her scotch and water with ice as she cries.*

VALERIE
(*crying*)

I was tall and I developed early. If that's a crime, go ahead and sue me, but I am not from trashy people.

MEL

No one's suggesting that.

VALERIE

Your daddy was poor. He worked in my father's liquor warehouse in Baton Rouge –

MEL

Was I conceived in Baton Rouge?

VALERIE

In the liquor warehouse, on the cement floor. Oh, my parents hated Lars.

MEL

My father's name is Lars?

Lars Waara.

MEL

What kind of name is Waara?

VALERIE

Finnish.

MEL
(*incredulous*)

I'm Finnish?

VALERIE

Finnish-American. And half Scottish-American.

MEL

God, what is that like? I don't know how to do that.

VALERIE *pulls out a wooden box and opens it, revealing a beautiful silver pendant.*

VALERIE

This belonged to my great-great-grandmamma, who was married to the Confederate general, Beauregard Clifford. I want you to have it.

She lifts the pendant carefully out of the box and puts it around NANCY*'s neck.*

NANCY

Are you sure? It's so beautiful.

VALERIE

He was an expert boxer and marksman.

MEL

What an athletic family.

VALERIE

I was on two championship basketball teams myself.

MEL

Why don't we name the baby Beauregard?

NANCY

Beauregard?

VALERIE

Oh, I'm so touched.

TINA

Damn, this camera is jammed again, and that was such a terrific moment.

They look at her. TINA *fusses with the camera.*

MEL

Let me take a look.

He takes the camera from TINA *and examines it.*

VALERIE

There's more light in the living room.

NANCY

I can't believe you're going to interrupt this for the camera.

MEL

We all want the tape, so let me handle this, please.

Leaves with TINA.

VALERIE

He's a very decisive man, isn't he?

CUT TO:

INT. VALERIE'S LIVING ROOM – DAY

A large, yellow and orange living room. MEL *and* TINA *stand by a big window while he holds the camera steady as she examines it.*

MEL

You come from a very athletic family, too, don't you?

He puts his glasses on. They stand close together to examine the camera.

TINA

My brothers were big jocks. There's a glob of gunk or something in there, see?

MEL

Oh, yeah. You've gotta get that off somehow.

                              TINA
Here. Let's use my skirt. It's old.

                              MEL
Really?

                              TINA
Yeah.

She hands the camera to MEL *then lifts up the hem of her little cotton miniskirt and starts employing an edge of it to clean the wheel.* MEL *is staring at her now completely exposed legs. She drops her skirt.*

Is it off? Mel?

He is staring at her legs.

                              MEL
What?

                              TINA
Can you tell if the wheel is clean?

He looks at the camera.

                              MEL
It's gone. How long did you say you were a dancer?

                              TINA
Don't remind me, I haven't been to the gym in months.

                              MEL
You don't need to go to the gym.

                              TINA
You're being very generous, but believe me, when I was a dancer, my calves didn't look like this.

She turns her calf.

                              MEL
They look pretty strong to me.

                              TINA
They were always strong. When I was little, I used to beat my brothers at Indian wrestling all the time.

                              41

CUT TO:

INT. VALERIE'S KITCHEN – DAY

NANCY *watches* VALERIE *sing.*

                    VALERIE
                 (*sings softly*)
I'm Beauregard from Dixie, Hoo-ray, hoo-ray!

                    NANCY
Technically, he's from New York.

                    VALERIE
                   (*sings*)
My name is Little Beauregard, and I come from the Land of
Dixie. Join in, Nancy.

   NANCY *joins in wanly.*

               VALERIE & NANCY
Look away, look away –
   CUT TO:

INT. VALERIE'S LIVING ROOM – DAY

MEL *and* TINA *stand with the outside of one foot pressed together, hands
locked in a handshake, trying to push each other off balance. They are
Indian wrestling.*

                    TINA
Feel it in your legs?

                    MEL
It's more about upper body strength, isn't it?

                    TINA
No, it's all in the legs.

                    MEL
How?

                    TINA
You'll see when you lose your balance.

She jerks her arm back. He loses his balance and goes flying past TINA *and knocks over a glass bookcase covered with delicate glass animals, smashing it all to the floor. He looks guilty as* NANCY *walks in with* VALERIE.

NANCY

What happened?

VALERIE

Oh, my Lord.

He gets up slowly and surveys the mess. TINA *stands there with her hand over her mouth in shock.*

MEL

I am so sorry.

NANCY

I don't know what's gotten into you.

VALERIE *kneels on the floor and picks up the remnants of her glass menagerie with a sad look on her face.*

VALERIE

My Chinese zodiac is ruined.

She picks up a stub of glass.

What happened to the head of my rooster?

MEL

Is that it?

VALERIE

No. That's the dog's pillow.

He chucks it to the side.

VALERIE

Don't throw it.

He gets onto his hands and knees to retrieve it.

MEL

I want to pay for all of this.

VALERIE

Absolutely not, it's out of the question.

MEL

Why?

VALERIE

All children break things and all children are forgiven, but you've never had that opportunity with me. So let's take this as a gift from God. Look –

She suddenly grabs a glass rabbit that is not broken.

It's another gift from God. The rabbit's still in one piece.

MEL

What do you mean?

VALERIE

Both you and your daddy are Year of the Rabbit.

MEL

I always thought I was the Year of the Dragon. At least on all those place mats in Chinese restaurants.

VALERIE

No, no. Lars is 1939 and you're 1963, and those are both Rabbit years. Trust me, I've been doing this a long time.

MEL

Actually, I was born in sixty-five.

VALERIE

Don't you think I know what year my own son was born?

TINA

Of course you do, Valerie.

MEL

You mean I'm two years older than I thought I was?

TINA

I can clear this up with one call to the office.

She pulls her cellular phone from a bag and dials a number as she leaves the room.

At that moment, two tall, six-foot-three-inch blond TWINS, *women, twenty-two years old, wearing bathing suits, walk in – as* TINA *continues to talk on the phone in the background. They are* JANE *and* SANDRA.

JANE

What happened to your glass animals?

The girls stare at the mess on the floor; they are holding a stack of new T-shirts.

VALERIE

These are the twins from my third marriage, Jane and Sandra. Say hello to your half brother, Mel.

SANDRA

Oh, man.

They start to giggle as they look at MEL.

VALERIE

What's so funny?

SANDRA

He looks like Uncle Freddie.

VALERIE
(*looks at Mel*)
Yes, he does. Why didn't I see that?

MEL
I'm flattered. What's Uncle Freddie like?

JANE
Really sweet-natured.

MEL
Great.

JANE
But he's a, what do you call it?

VALERIE
Frotteurist.

SANDRA
Yeah, he's a frotteurist.

MEL
What's that?

SANDRA
You rub up against people in crowded public places.

NANCY
Mel used to do that.

MEL
She's kidding.

VALERIE
It's not something to joke about.

SANDRA
Yeah, he went to jail for it.

MEL
Oh.

JANE
Can he come down to the beach?

VALERIE

He doesn't have time for that, Jane.

JANE

Why not?

SANDRA

We're in the volleyball finals.

MEL

Wow. That's impressive.

JANE

You can wear one of our shirts.

SANDRA

Yeah, give him a shirt.

MEL

You have team shirts?

They lead MEL *to the stack of shirts on the pool table.*

Thanks. This is great. Let's go down to the beach with them, Nancy.

TINA
(*re-enters*)

I don't believe this, but there's been a terrible, terrible mistake.

They all look at her.

Valerie's not your mother, Mel.

MEL

Of course she's my mother. We've got the same forehead.

JANE

And he looks like Uncle Freddie.

MEL

Yeah, I look like Uncle Freddie.

TINA

Please don't make this any harder on yourself than it already is.

VALERIE

Are you positive?

NANCY

How could you make a mistake like that?

TINA

Our computer files were in transition, and Valerie's son is named Martin Coplin, and he lives in Orlando, Florida. Mel's father is named –

She consults her pad.

Fritz Boudreau. He lives in Gundall, Michigan. I feel like a complete idiot.

NANCY

We flew all the way out here. We have this big emotional reunion –

TINA

Go on, get it out. We'll all feel better.

NANCY

Are you humoring me?

TINA

I'm not humoring you. I'm serious.

VALERIE

I expect you to pay for this damage.

MEL

You said it was a gift from God.

VALERIE

That was when you were my son.

MEL

Don't you have insurance?

VALERIE

And raise my premiums? No, thank you. (*sticks her hand out*) I'd like my pendant back.

NANCY *takes the pendant off and gives it to* VALERIE, *who leaves the room.* NANCY *pauses, then takes the* BABY *from* MEL *and leaves*

49

the room. TINA *exits the opposite way to go to the bathroom, looking distraught.* MEL *is left alone with the* TWINS.

                              SANDRA
Can we have our shirt back?

She takes the T-shirt from MEL.

                              JANE
We'd let you keep it, but we don't have very many of them.

                              MEL
I understand.

                              SANDRA
Sorry.

They stand for an awkward moment, and then the TWINS *leave.*
MEL *stands alone in the living room.*
CUT TO:

EXT. VALERIE'S HOUSE – DAY

MEL *and* NANCY, *and* TINA *walk to the car that is parked on the street and stand looking disoriented until* TINA *breaks the ice.*

                              TINA
Once we get over the disappointment and shock, I think we can look at this as a good dry run.

                              MEL
Yeah, I think it loosened me up for the real thing.

NANCY *shakes her head as they get into the car.*
CUT TO:

EXT. MOTEL – SAN DIEGO – NIGHT
CUT TO:

INT. MOTEL ROOM – NIGHT

NANCY *stands at the dresser and pours hot water from a kettle into a mug.* MEL *sits on the bed with articles spread around him. The* BABY *sleeps in the bassinet next to the bed.*

50

I can't believe that gigantic woman had me singing 'Dixie.'

MEL

I was so caught up in everything I just went blind to how weird they were.

NANCY *walks over to him.*

*[NANCY

That Reagan remark really took me off guard.

MEL

I was trying to be open to them.

NANCY

You don't have to be that open. You want to become a Republican frotteurist or something?

MEL

I never even heard that word before today.

NANCY

Close your eyes for a frotteurist surprise.

MEL

You want me to close my eyes?

NANCY

Yes.

He closes his eyes. She fills her mouth with the warm water while he waits with his eyes closed, and she disappears between his legs, her cheeks full of water.

MEL
(*opens his eyes*)

What are you doing?

NANCY

Mm hmm mum mum.

MEL

You look like a chipmunk.

*Cut from completed film

She sits up and spits the water back into the glass.

NANCY

I told you to keep your eyes closed.

MEL

Is that hot water? You could scald me.

NANCY

It's not that hot. Jill said she does this all the time.

MEL

Are you swapping sex secrets with Jill?

NANCY
(*goes to the bathroom*)

Are we ever going to make love again?

MEL

We're just rusty because of the baby.

NANCY

This started before the baby.

MEL

Maybe we need a little novelty to stir things up.

NANCY
(*calls from bathroom*)

That was novelty. The warm water was novelty.

MEL

I don't mean weird stunts, I don't know what I mean. I'm
preoccupied with this trip, that's all. Don't panic about it.]

She steps aggressively out of the bathroom wearing a shower cap.

NANCY

How did you knock over those glass shelves, anyway?

MEL

At Valerie's?

NANCY

Yes.

MEL

We were working on the camera and we backed into it.

NANCY

It seems strange that you would just happen to back into it.

MEL

OK, we were Indian wrestling.

NANCY

Indian wrestling? What's that?

MEL

It's this stupid thing kids do.

NANCY

Why were you doing it?

MEL

We were talking about my athletic family, or Valerie's athletic family, which I thought was my athletic family, and then Tina's athletic family –

NANCY
(paces)

You're attracted to her, aren't you?

MEL

No.

NANCY

It's OK. She's an attractive woman.

MEL

Of course she's attractive, but I'm married to you.

NANCY

Married to me or in love with me?

MEL

Come on, Nancy, don't do this.

NANCY
(returns to bathroom)

She may be attractive, but let me tell you, she's got a screw loose somewhere.

53

MEL

(*calls after her*)

I'll grant you she's a little eccentric, but I wouldn't worry about it, and I'm definitely in love with you.

CUT TO:

CLOSE UP: *Freight train or semi passing by, to reveal –*

EXT. CAR – INDUSTRIAL MICHIGAN – DAY

Another white rental car. TINA *drives.* MEL *sits in the passenger seat.* NANCY *sits in back with the* BABY.

Outside it is an industrial wasteland of oil storage tanks, railroad tracks, and high tension wires. The sky is overcast and gray. The rental car pulls up to a shotgun shack next to the railroad tracks. There is a big semi truck parked next to the little house.

They all get out of the car as a short freight train rattles by the house and passes. TINA *pulls out the camcorder and follows* MEL.

TINA

(*taping*)

Well, this looks *muy macho*, doesn't it?

NANCY

It seems a little creepy to me.

The door of the little house opens behind them.

TINA

Look, someone's coming out.

MEL *and* NANCY *turn to see* TWO MEN *emerging from the shotgun shack. One is average height, the other is short, about five-six.*

They look rather gruff as they come down the cracked cement path to the big semi rig. The short one wears a leather vest with a chain on it; the tall one wears an old denim jacket and carries a gym bag. MEL *runs across the snowy/muddy front yard toward the two men.*

MEL

Excuse me –

The two men stop by the cab of the semi and look at MEL *as he walks*

54

up. TINA *and* NANCY *watch from a distance.* NANCY *holds the* BABY .

Hi.

The men eye MEL *suspiciously.*

Is one of you Fritz Boudreau?

FRITZ

Who wants to know?

MEL

Mel Coplin –

FRITZ *shoves* MEL *hard, knocking him backwards.*

FRITZ

Did I invite you onto my property?

MEL

Take it easy.

TINA *comes up with the camcorder, followed by* NANCY.

NANCY

Don't go over there, Tina.

NANCY *watches as* TINA *approaches* MEL *and the two men. The big one grabs the camcorder from* TINA*'s hands and smashes it to the ground and stomps on it.*

TINA
(bends for camera)

Let me explain –

The big one kicks the camera away as she tries to pick it up.

Will you relax? We can talk about this.

TINA *pulls a small tape recorder from her bag.*

(into tape recorder)

Test, test, test –

MITCH *tries to take it but she won't give it up. They wrestle over it.*

55

MEL

What's happening?

TINA *wrenches it away and* MITCH *grabs her shoulder.*

TINA

Fuck. Run.

TINA *runs into the truck yard.* MEL *and* NANCY *hesitate, looking at* FRITZ, *then they run also.*

NANCY
(*pointing, running*)

The car's over there. Wait.

FRITZ *and* MITCH *catch them and grab* MEL *and* TINA *loosely by their coats.*

MEL
(*to Tina*)

Doesn't he want to meet me?

TINA

I felt bad about San Diego, so I bent the rules a little.

MEL

You didn't even call him.

TINA

That's not true. I tried to call, but his phone doesn't work.

FRITZ

What the fuck do you people want?

MEL

We just want to know if one of you is Fritz Boudreau, because they said he's my father.

FRITZ

Who said I'm your father?

MEL

She did.

TINA

The Maidstone Adoption Agency.

56

FRITZ

They said you're my son? My son?

MEL

Yeah. I'm your son.

FRITZ
(warmly)

You little shit.

He suddenly embraces MEL *in a nuggy head lock.*

Look at this little turd, Mitch. This turd is my son. I'm sorry, man, did we scare you?

MEL

A little, yeah.

FRITZ

I'm sorry. We were scared, too. We didn't know who you were.
(*lets go of* MEL)
I spread a lot of baby batter in my day, but this is the first son I ever met.

TINA

This is so great, I wish I had my camcorder.

MITCH

I'm sorry about that. Cameras freak me out.

TINA

That's OK, I rushed into this without thinking.

FRITZ

You picked a helluva time to drop by, turd face.

FRITZ *affectionately puts his fist on* MEL *'s chest.*

MEL
(*blocking his face from punches*)
She said your phone doesn't work.

FRITZ
(*new headlock, speaks warmly*)
Now, I don't need no son to give me a guilt trip about a phone.

57

MITCH

We got to get going, Fritz.

FRITZ

Oh, shit. Yeah.

MEL

You have to go somewhere?

FRITZ

We gotta get our wheels balanced for a big trip tomorrow. Sorry.

MEL

When are you coming back?

FRITZ

After Eugene balances the wheels, we head out for three weeks.

MEL

Bad timing, I guess.

FRITZ

Damn it. Bad timing.

MITCH

Wait. Why don't you come to Eugene's? He's only twenty minutes away.

FRITZ

Yeah, come with us.

MEL

In the truck?

FRITZ

Yeah. You ever been in a truck before?

MEL

Not really.

FRITZ

We'll get you back to your car before supper time.

TINA

Really?

                    MITCH
Sure.

                    MEL
OK.

                    NANCY
Maybe it's better if we meet when you get back from your trip.

                    MEL
No, I don't want to put this off.

                    TINA
                (to Nancy)
You can meet us later, if you want. It's up to you.

  NANCY *stares at* TINA.
  CUT TO:

INT. CAB OF FRITZ'S SEMI — DAY

The truck rolls through the industrial area. FRITZ *drives.* MITCH *sits in the passenger seat.* MEL *sits in the middle.* TINA, NANCY, *and the* BABY *sit in the back. They all must shout to be heard over the engine.*

                    MEL
              (shouts over engine)
This is great.

                    TINA
Fabulous, Mr Boudreau.

                    FRITZ
A lot of people look down on drivers like we're low-class.

                    MEL
Not me. I always wanted to learn how to drive a big truck.

                    NANCY
You never told me that.

                    MEL
I may not have realized it until now, but I think it's always been a fantasy of mine.

                                        FRITZ
You want a lesson?

                                        MEL
You'd give me a lesson?

                                        FRITZ
Sure, why not?

                                        MITCH
That's gonna slow us down.

                                        FRITZ
No boy of mine is gonna slow us down, Mitch.

                                        NANCY
Let's not do this while the baby's in the truck.

                                        FRITZ
Don't you trust me?

                                        NANCY
Of course I trust you, but he's never done this before.

                                        MITCH
She's not gonna let him drive, so forget about it.

                                        FRITZ
Are you saying my son's a bitch boy?

                                        MITCH
I'm not saying that.

                                        FRITZ
What's your name again?

                                        MEL
Mel.

                                        FRITZ
You ain't no bitch boy, are you, Mel?

                                        MEL
No, I don't believe I am a bitch boy.

                         NANCY
Don't let him bait you into doing something stupid, Mel.

                         TINA
Mel needs your support, Nancy.

                         MEL
Yeah, I need support, honey.

                         FRITZ
                    (*raises his hand*)
I support you, Mel.

                         MITCH
                    (*raises hand*)
Me, too.

                         NANCY
I want to get out. You're acting like an asshole.

                    FRITZ & MITCH
Oooohhh. Pussy-whipped.

EXT. RURAL POST OFFICE – DAY

The truck pulls into the small parking lot around a tiny clapboard post office. NANCY *gets out of the truck and stands by the little post office as she holds the* BABY.
CUT TO:

INT. FRITZ'S SEMI CAB – DAY

MEL *sits in the driver's seat.* FRITZ *coaches him from the passenger's seat.* TINA *and* MITCH *sit in back.*

                         TINA
OK, now what are all these wonderful things here –

                         FRITZ
This here's your clutch –

                         MEL
And this is the brake –

FRITZ

No, that's clutch number two.

MEL *looks confusedly at all the pedals.*

Hey, you know what? You got a kind of Jew look to you, don't you?

MEL

The people who raised me were Jewish.

MITCH

They gave you a kike look, didn't they?

MEL

Don't say that. That's not nice.

FRITZ

Wait a second. It's not a Jew face. It's a face like Old Needledick's, isn't it?

MITCH

Yeah.

MITCH *touches* MEL*'s nose;* MEL *brushes his hand off.*

MEL

Who's Old Needledick?

MITCH

You ain't into science by any chance, are you?

MEL

I'm an entymologist, actually.

MITCH

E-N-T-Y-M-O-L-O-G-I-S-T. Sounds like a scientist to me.

MEL

What exactly are you saying?

FRITZ

When I met your mother, I was riding with the Angels out of Oakland, Cal.

                              MEL

Hell's Angels?

                              FRITZ

Yeah, and we got invited to these fancy parties because rich people
wanted to hang around with the Angels and all the musical bands
and what not. And your mother meets this scientist guy Richard
Schlich – something, I never could pronounce it right.

                              MITCH

S-C-H-L-I-C-H-T-I-N-G.

                              MEL

So she met this guy –

                              FRITZ

Right and they ran off to Antelope Wells together, and I never was
sure who sired that baby.

                              MEL

Are you saying you're not sure you're my father?

                              TINA

This can't be happening again.
    CUT TO:

EXT. RURAL POST OFFICE – DAY

NANCY *holds the* BABY *and watches as the back of the semi trailer
touches the corner of the clapboard post office.*

                              NANCY

Hey. You're going to hit the building.

    The truck continues and starts to touch the pillar.

Hey.
    CUT TO:

INT. FRITZ'S SEMI CAB – DAY

                              TINA

The records show that you brought him into the agency.

FRITZ

I did a good deed as a favor because his mother and father were indisposed.

MEL

Indisposed how?

FRITZ

You'd have to ask her that.

TINA

But we don't know where she is.
CUT TO:

EXT. POST OFFICE – DAY

The semi has stopped.

NANCY

OK, good. Now just pull forward.
CUT TO:

INT. FRITZ'S SEMI CAB – DAY

TINA

Look, isn't it possible she was pregnant when she left you?

FRITZ

Not with that face and the science thing –

MITCH

Hey, I think we're rolling backwards here.

MEL

What should I do?

FRITZ

Just like your old man: so intellectual, but so dumb.

MEL

Which one's the brake?

FRITZ

Which one's the brake? Why am I here? Who's my father?

                              MEL

Just tell me what to do.

                             FRITZ

No. Figure it out yourself, Mr Big Shot Scientist. You and your
father think you're so fucking smart and superior –

                              MEL

I do not think I'm superior –

                             FRITZ

Oh, yes, you do.

                              TINA
                         (*shifts down*)

Just put it in first –

> *The truck jerks backward.*
> CUT TO:

EXT. RURAL POST OFFICE

The semi lunges further into the post office, crushing it even more.
NANCY *looks stunned.*
    CUT TO:

LATER

The semi sits lodged in the little old wooden post office. FRITZ *and*
MITCH *are being led away in handcuffs by two* COPS, *while* TINA, *also
in handcuffs, runs after* FRITZ. *A firetruck could be in the background.*

                             FRITZ

Hey, you can tell your mother this wouldn'ta happened if you were
my son. You'd know how to drive a truck, you fucking bitch boy.

                              TINA
                    (*running after* FRITZ)

Where's Antelope Wells?

                              COP

Step away, ma'am.

TINA
(*turns to cops*)
Do you know where Antelope Wells is?

Another COP *walks by and she follows him.*

Excuse me, do you know where Antelope Wells is?
CUT TO:

INT. SECURITY OFFICE – NIGHT

It is a spare room with a table and chairs and a one-way mirror on one wall. TINA *paces and looks agitated as she smokes a cigarette.* NANCY *paces with the* BABY. MEL *sits, looking miserable.*

NANCY
'I don't need to be criticized. I need support right now. If he wants to drive the truck, let him drive the truck.'

MEL
I think you've made your point.

NANCY
You expect me to get on a plane to New Mexico now?

The door opens and two FEDERAL AGENTS *walk in wearing grey suits, white shirts, and dark ties. They are both trim and athletic-looking. One is about forty, white, with blue eyes. This is* PAUL. *The other is about twenty-eight, dark. This is* TONY.

PAUL
Agent Paul Harmon, Bureau of Alcohol, Tobacco, and Firearms. This is Agent Tony Kent.

TONY, *the younger agent, nods.*

Let's see here, you thought this man Fritz Boudreau was your father, but in fact, he is not your father?

NANCY
Oh, my God, Tony?

He looks at her with stunned recognition.

Tony Kent?

66

TONY
(*removes sunglasses*)

Nancy Curwin?

NANCY

This is unbelievable. We both went to high school in Chicago.

TONY

You look fantastic.

NANCY

No, I'm exhausted and I need a shower. What are you doing in this police job?

TONY

My cousin got it for me. I need a health plan while I'm trying to write my book. What are you doing now?

NANCY

Curating.

TONY

Wow.

PAUL

Excuse me, but we've got a problem to take care of.

TONY

I'm, sorry, Paul. Go ahead.

PAUL *walks up to* MEL *and hands him his license.*

PAUL

It's a federal offense to destroy a United States post office.

MEL

It's not like it was a premeditated act of terrorism.

PAUL

I'll be the judge of that. Now, the ostensible purpose of this truck ride was what exactly?

TONY
(*takes the* BABY)

The baby's beautiful; he looks a lot like you.

NANCY

Thank you.

PAUL

Tony.

TONY

Just for a minute. Look at that hair.

PAUL

Give the baby back.

TONY

Feel his little grip, Paul, it's really strong.

PAUL

Jesus Christ.

PAUL *throws down his notebook on the table, knocking a glass to the floor. Everyone looks uncomfortable.*

TONY

You're under way too much stress.

PAUL

The man drove a semi into a federal building.

TONY

He's Nancy Curwin's husband. It was an accident.

MEL

It's Nancy Coplin now.

TONY

How long have you been married?

PAUL

Hey. There are procedures that have to be followed.

TONY

He's got a valid license, doesn't he?

PAUL

Not to drive a truck.

TONY

It was the trucker's fault for letting him drive in the first place.

PAUL

Could I talk to you privately, please?

He opens the door. TONY *walks out, followed by* PAUL, *who closes the door.* MEL, NANCY, *and* TINA *listen uncomfortably as* PAUL *berates* TONY *outside the room.*

PAUL
(*off screen*)

I am in charge of this investigation.

TONY
(*off screen*)

You don't have to suspend his license.

PAUL
(*off screen*)

You've got to start taking this job more seriously.

CUT TO:

INT. CORRIDOR OUTSIDE ROOM – NIGHT

TONY

Don't embarrass me in front of my friends.

PAUL

Don't embarrass me on the job, goddamn it.

TONY

Look at you. Would you breathe, please?

PAUL *breathes.*

The door opens. PAUL *and* TONY *come back in.*

PAUL

It looks like this Boudreau fellow's going to take the heat for letting you drive, but if you get behind the wheel of another truck, you'll lose your license for sure.

NANCY

Is that it? Are we free to go?

PAUL

Yes, you're free to go.

TONY

Do you have a place to stay tonight?

TINA

We'll probably go to a motel.

PAUL

Don't do that. There are so many wonderful B and Bs right here on Lake Michigan.

MEL

I hate B and Bs.

PAUL

Why do you hate B and Bs?

MEL

First of all, there's no privacy –

70

PAUL

No privacy?

MEL

You have to share a bathroom, you have to make chit-chat with
the boring old lady –

PAUL

That's what makes it fun.

MEL

There's always some old cat walking around, you have to pretend
you like the cat.

TINA

Whatever we do, I have to eat something because I'm starving.

TONY

Why don't you let us take you out to dinner?

PAUL

What are you, apologizing for the arrest?

TONY

No, I want to catch up with Nancy. We can take them to
Minetti's.

PAUL

Oh, Minetti's is great.
                    (looks at watch)
You'll never get a reservation this late.

MEL

That's very nice of you, but we'll be fine on our own.

PAUL

Yeah, Tony, we don't want to intrude.

NANCY

Don't be silly. We're getting sick of each other's company.

MEL *looks at her.*

                              TONY
                          (*to* PAUL)
See? It's fine.
    CUT TO:

INT. MINETTI'S RESTAURANT – MICHIGAN – NIGHT

They are done eating. MEL *is not at the table.* TONY *and* NANCY *are
playing with the* BABY, *who is bouncing on* TONY's *lap.*

                              PAUL
Antelope Wells is tucked in the south-eastern corner of New
Mexico.

                             NANCY
Have you been there?

                              PAUL
I've been near there. You've got White Sands National
Monument in the area, and there's a fantastic hot springs not
many people know about.

                             NANCY
I almost wish you could come and show me around while Mel
meets his family.

                              TONY
You've got the personal days, Paul, you should do it.

                              PAUL
No, I can't leave work right now.

    MEL *walks up and sits down at the table.*

                              MEL
Unbelievable line at the bathroom.

                              PAUL
It's always that way here. They should get a bigger bathroom.

                              TONY
                      (*bouncing the* BABY)
Look at that smile.

NANCY
(*laughing*)

He loves you, Tony. You're wonderful with babies.

TONY

I want one of these so badly. Do you think you could help me with
an adoption, Tina?

TINA

That depends on the specifics of your situation.

TONY

Like what?

TINA

Number one: are you married?

TONY

Yes.

TINA

Does your spouse work?

TONY

Yes.

TINA

Is she willing to adopt?

TONY

That's where the snag is.

TINA

Then you've got a real problem.

TONY

What are my chances as a single parent?

PAUL *stands up suddenly. He looks very upset.*

PAUL

Excuse me.

MEL *leans forward so he can get by.*

73

TONY

Why can't you stay and discuss this?

PAUL

Because I happen to believe in privacy, that's why.

TONY

We have nothing to be ashamed of.

PAUL

I don't believe in sharing my personal life with everyone I meet, OK?

TONY

This isn't just anyone, she works at an adoption agency, and I thought she could be helpful.

PAUL *walks off. They all stare at* TONY, *somewhat stunned, as they realize that* TONY *and* PAUL *are a couple.*

I keep telling him that a baby will reduce stress by taking his mind off work, but he just doesn't listen.

MEL, TINA, *and* NANCY *stare at* TONY *as he bounces the* BABY *on his knee. He turns to* MEL.

So where did you folks come down on the big circumcision controversy? There's a movement afoot to keep the foreskin these days, but, personally, I think a boy's penis should look just like his father's.

They all look at him.

MEL
(*reaches forward*)

Could I have the baby, please?

They all look at him.
CUT TO:

INT. B AND B LIVING ROOM – MICHIGAN – NIGHT

It is a dark, Victorian living room with one lamp on, as MEL, NANCY *and* TINA *listen politely to an* OLD WOMAN *in glasses.*

74

OLD WOMAN

Of course that was back in 1957, when there were no other
buildings along this beach. My late husband devised his own anti-
erosion system with simple two-by-fours positioned in a zigzag
system that we later patented, thanks to the advice of a dear friend
who was in a law firm with Gerald Ford. My brother has the same
birthday as President Ford, who's a very sweet man. We met him
twice.

A big, old cat hisses at them as it lumbers by.
CUT TO:

INT. B AND B BEDROOM – NIGHT

MEL changes the BABY*'s diaper on the bed while* NANCY *unpacks with
a bathing cap on her head, preparing for a shower. She wears a
kimono.*

MEL
(*changing diaper*)

Why couldn't we go to a motel? Because at a motel, you don't get
the bonus of someone related to Gerald Ford's birthday –

NANCY

Birthday – Oh, my God. We forgot your father's birthday.

They stand and look at each other.
CUT TO:

INT. B AND B KITCHEN – NIGHT

MEL holds the phone to his ear and looks around the kitchen guiltily.

MRS COPLIN
(*off screen*)

Hello?

MEL
(*whispering*)

It's me, Mom.
CUT TO:

INT. MR AND MRS COPLIN'S DINING ROOM – NIGHT

They sit at a table set for three more, including a baby place setting.
They have obviously eaten alone.

MRS COPLIN

How's the psychic healing going?

MEL

I'm sorry we didn't make it back for Dad's birthday.

MRS COPLIN
(low key)

That's all right. We can try it again when he turns sixty-five,
provided he lives that long and you're not too busy.

MEL
(whispers)

I said I was sorry.

MRS COPLIN

Why are you whispering?

MEL
(whispering)

I'm not supposed to be using this phone.

MRS COPLIN

Are you all right?

MEL
(anxiously)

There was a big mix up in San Diego, and then the truck flattened
a post office in Michigan –

MRS COPLIN

What truck?

MR COPLIN

What happened with a truck?

MEL

It's fine, we have the right information now and we're going to
New Mexico.

76

MRS COPLIN

New Mexico? I thought you were in San Diego.

MR COPLIN

Tell him there's uranium in the water down there.

MRS COPLIN

Will you shush? He's in some kind of trouble. Did your car get bumped in San Diego?

MEL

There was a minor incident, oh, no, I have to go –

He looks panicked as the OLD WOMAN *walks into the kitchen, carrying her cat. The* OLD WOMAN *walks up to* MEL.

OLD WOMAN

No, no we don't do this here unless it's an emergency.

MEL

Yes, it's an emergency.

OLD WOMAN

The kitchen is verboten at night.

MRS COPLIN

What's the emergency?

OLD WOMAN

Do you need an ambulance? Is it the baby?

MRS COPLIN

Oh, God, what's wrong with the baby?

MEL

The baby's fine.

OLD WOMAN

Hang up.

MRS COPLIN

Don't try to protect me from this, Mel. Do you need help?

MEL

Things aren't going very well –

OLD WOMAN

Do you see that sign? You have to use the pay phone at the gas station after eight p.m.

MEL

Give me thirty seconds.

OLD WOMAN

You want to pay my phone bill? Hang up.

MRS COPLIN

Is that tyrant your mother?

MEL
(into phone)
I have to go, Mom, but we're going to be with the Schlichtings –

MRS COPLIN

Their name is Shitkings?

MEL

The Schlichtings, my parents.

MR COPLIN

What kind of name is Shitking?

MRS COPLIN
(into phone)
What kind of name is Shitking?

OLD WOMAN
(shouts, red faced)
Verboten means verboten!

MEL
(into phone)
I think it might be German, but we'll be in Antelope Wells and then –

The OLD WOMAN pushes the button down, hanging up the phone.

OLD WOMAN

Leave the kitchen immediately.

MEL

I used my calling card.

OLD WOMAN
(*shouts*)

That is not the point!

She holds the hissing cat up to MEL*'s face.*
CUT TO:

INT. MR & MRS COPLIN'S DINING ROOM – NIGHT

MRS COPLIN

Hello? Mel?

She hangs up.

MR COPLIN

What happened?

MRS COPLIN

He got cut off.

MR COPLIN

Is he in trouble?

MRS COPLIN

God, Eddie, something terrible is happening to him.

MR COPLIN
(*puts arm around her*)

Calm down. What did he say?

MRS COPLIN

I can't calm down, we have to do something.

MR COPLIN

All right, we'll call back.

MRS COPLIN

We can't call back, he's going to New Mexico, for God's sake.

MR COPLIN
(*worried*)

Who knows what kind of people he's with? Anything is possible.

MRS COPLIN

Don't say that, you're scaring me.

MR COPLIN

No, I'm not. You're already scared.

MRS COPLIN

I was not.

MR COPLIN

Yes, you were.

MRS COPLIN

We have to do something.

CUT TO:

INT. B AND B BEDROOM – NIGHT

It is a frilly Victorian bedroom, with old oriental carpeting and antique furniture. The BABY *sleeps in a bassinet.*

NANCY *sits on the bed in a nightie, putting lotion on her legs and arms. She is fresh from the shower and wears a bathing cap and a towel.*

The door opens and MEL *walks in, looking pissed, and slams the door.*

NANCY

Did you call your parents?

He starts to take his shoes and pants off.

MEL

I almost got mauled by the merry innkeeper.

NANCY

The kitchen's off limits after eight.

MEL

What are you, her spy? You're the one who told me to call.

NANCY

I thought you'd use Tina's phone.

MEL

Her phone doesn't work here.

NANCY

You're feeling frustrated.

He sits heavily on the bed.

MEL

Yes, I'm feeling frustrated.

NANCY

I told you your expectations were too high for all of this.

MEL

Maybe it's time to pack it up and go home.

NANCY

Don't start that. You always get pessimistic when you're close to finishing something.

MEL

I do?

NANCY

You did it about the apartment, about the wedding, about the pregnancy.

MEL

You're right. I always do that.

NANCY

Stick to your plan for once, OK?

MEL

Thanks.

He kisses her on the cheek, picks up his toiletry bag, and leaves.
CUT TO:

INT. B AND B HALLWAY – NIGHT

It is the dimly lit upstairs floor of an old Victorian house, with quaint old carpeting.

MEL *comes down the hall and walks up to the closed bathroom door just as there is a flushing inside. The door opens.*

TINA *emerges and walks right into* MEL. *She wears panties and a camisole. Her face is red, and she has been crying.*

*[MEL

What's wrong?

TINA

This divorce hits me in waves, you know what I mean? The loneliness and the loss sneak up on me late at night. It's horrible.

MEL

I'm sure it's very painful.

TINA

You share you life with someone, but you feel trapped so you get out, and then it's so horrible you wonder if you should've stayed.]

She blows her nose in a tissue.

This trip hasn't worked out the way I wanted it to. I owe you an apology.

MEL

I'm sure it's going to be fine. We've just had a few unexpected bumps.

TINA

You're such an optimist. Where does that come from?

MEL

I've always said it's a mistake to let pessimism take over when you're about to finish something.

TINA

That's the complete opposite of my ex-husband. Anyway, good night.

She kisses him gently on the cheek, brushing her body against his. They smile at each other.

MEL

Good night.

*Cut from completed film

TINA

Good night.

They kiss again lightly on the lips, then suddenly kiss deeply and embrace each other, running their hands up and down each other's bodies hungrily. TINA*'s toiletry bag spills onto the floor as they grope.*

Just as suddenly, they break apart, glazed with sex and embarrassment. TINA *looks very troubled as she gathers her toiletries. She turns, embarrassed, and walks quickly down the hall.* MEL *stands and watches her disappear into her room. Then he turns and goes back to his room, skipping the bathroom altogether.*
CUT TO:

INT. B AND B BEDROOM – NIGHT

MEL *comes back in and closes the door. There is a pup tent in his boxers, which he tries to conceal.*

NANCY

What are you doing? Have you got a pup tent in there?

She looks at the pup tent. He gets onto the bed next to her. She looks at him.

MEL

I'm feeling very sexual for some reason.

NANCY

Were there some sexy magazines in the bathroom or something?

She watches him with dismay as he comes over and begins ravenously kissing and caressing her. He presses her down on the bed. She laughs. She looks at him as he is pulling up her nightgown, and his eyes are closed.

(*laughing*)

Honey, wait.

He doesn't stop. She tries to look at him, but he turns away.

Why aren't you looking at me?

He finally stops and sits up.

Maybe it's not natural for two people to stay together their entire lives. I mean, fifty years with the same person, how do people do it?

*[NANCY
(*deeply hurt*)

Am I that boring to you?

MEL

No, but a little variety might keep things from getting so claustrophobic.

NANCY

What's going on with you?

MEL

Don't you ever have these thoughts? Don't you want to sleep with other people?]

NANCY

Oh, I get it. Your parents aren't good enough, and now I'm not good enough because Tina's some fucking skinny dancer.

MEL

That's not what it's about. Jesus.

NANCY

It takes some women a year to get back to their normal weight after having a baby.

There is a sharp knocking on the door.

OLD WOMAN
(*shouts off screen*)

You're not good B and B people.

NANCY *walks away from* MEL *angrily, and out of frame.*
CUT TO:

*Cut from completed film

INT. MICHIGAN AIRPORT GATE – DAY

MEL *and* TINA *are waiting to hand their tickets to a* FLIGHT ATTENDANT *as they board the plane.* TINA *wears sunglasses and looks hungover. She takes out a cigarette, looks upset as she puts it into her mouth.* MEL *takes her lighter from her and lights it for her.*

> TINA

Listen, we have to talk.

> MEL

I'm feeling just as confused as you are.

> TINA

I'm not sure I need an affair with a married man right now.

> MEL

Could you keep your voice down?

> TINA

I'm in the middle of a divorce, I'm going to school at night. I need to be taken seriously as a woman, I want to have children.

> MEL

I take you very seriously.

> TINA
> (*sniffling*)

You do?

> MEL

Yeah.

> TINA

Shit.

She suddenly turns and boards the plane.

NANCY *walks up behind* MEL *with the* BABY.

> NANCY

What's the matter with her?

> MEL

She's upset about the way things are going. Look, I probably owe you an apology for last night, but you can't expect every time we have sex to be some major love connection.

> NANCY

That doesn't sound like an apology.

> PAUL *and* TONY *come running up with tickets in their hands. They are dressed casually in jeans and colorful sportscoats.*

> TONY
> (*smiling*)

Hello, again, strangers.

> PAUL
> (*smiling*)

I'm sorry I stormed off like that last night. I suffer from hypertension, as you probably can tell.

> TONY

The whole thing was a blessing, actually, because it finally made Paul realize how much he needs some R and R, and I've never seen New Mexico.

> PAUL

Sometimes I need to get konked on the head, what can I say?

> MEL

You're coming to New Mexico?

> PAUL
> (*smiling*)

Nothing like the cruel acceptance of a casual invitation, is there?

> MEL

I don't recall any invitation.

> NANCY

I think you were in the bathroom.

> TONY

Oops. Did we jump the gun here?

> NANCY

No, it's fine, we'll be fine.

MEL

What do you mean, it's fine?

PAUL

We're just going to do some sightseeing. We won't be in the way.

NANCY

I'd love to have the company. It'll be fun.

TONY

I'll see if I can get an empty row for the baby.

NANCY

Terrific.

PAUL *and* TONY *board the plane.*

I'm sorry. I didn't expect this to happen.

MEL

You just had a little hostility to work out.

NANCY

This isn't hostile. I barely mentioned the idea to them –

MEL

Fine. Whatever.

NANCY

Don't get into a victim role here.

NANCY *leaves* MEL *alone at the gate, looking agitated.*
CUT TO:

INT. AIRPLANE – DAY

TONY *and* NANCY *sit in an empty row of seats as she nurses the* BABY, *exposing too much of her breasts as* TONY *watches.*

TONY

You know I couldn't be circumcised 'til I was a year old.

NANCY

Really? How come?

TONY

I had hypospadia, which is a curvature of the penis. It's fine now.

MEL looks annoyed as he stands and gives NANCY a big, cloth diaper.

MEL

Here, cover yourself up.

NANCY takes the diaper and puts it aside. MEL leaves.

NANCY

Ouch.

TONY

How's the irritation from nursing?

NANCY

Pretty bad, actually.

TONY

That's because you're not holding him at the right angle.

NANCY

Don't you think I know what I'm doing?

TONY

Just tell me if this feels better –

He moves the BABY, touches her breast.

NANCY

How did you get to be such an expert?

TONY

I used to date this woman who was a midwife. Doesn't that feel better?

NANCY

Actually, it does.

TONY

He was pulling down too much. You have beautiful breasts.

NANCY

Thank you.

TONY

I remember them from high school, not that I ever saw them –

He continues to handle the breast and the BABY. PAUL *walks up with two glasses of water.*

PAUL

Hi.

TONY

Would you mind finding another seat, Paul?

PAUL

Another seat?

TONY
(*takes the glasses*)
It would really help us out here with the baby.

PAUL

Sure, OK.

PAUL *looks a bit troubled as he walks off.*

NANCY
(*smiles*)
Thanks a million.

CUT TO:

MEL *and* TINA *sit side by side holding hands secretly. They stop when* PAUL *comes up and sits irritably in the empty seat next to* TINA.

PAUL

Is there something I should know about this trip that I haven't been clued into yet?

MEL *and* TINA *look at him.*

MEL

Would you mind sitting somewhere else?

PAUL
(*gets up*)
That's wonderful, that's just great. I can't believe how naïve I am.

CUT TO:

EXT. CAR RENTAL LOT — ALBUQUERQUE AIRPORT — DAY

Mountains and the open sky are in the background of the rental parking lot.

MEL and TINA walk down the line of rental cars and stop at a white Taurus rental in a line of white Taurus rentals.

TONY comes walking up briskly followed by PAUL and NANCY.

> NANCY
> Does anybody actually own a white Taurus, or are they all rentals?

> TONY
> Are you kidding? This is the most reliable mid-size in America, according to all the big reports.

> PAUL
> I'm feeling very depressed and I'd like to talk about what's happening, please.

> TONY
> What are you depressed about?

> PAUL
> I feel like there's an agenda here. It's not what I had in mind.

> NANCY
> What agenda?

> PAUL
> Do I have to spell it out? I'm obviously the fifth wheel here. What do you think that feels like?

> TONY
> We're riding in two cars until we get to the B and B, Paul, that's not an agenda.

> MEL
> Let's just hit the road, OK?

> NANCY
> Do you mind if Paul rides with you?

> MEL
> Why can't he go with you?

                              PAUL
Do you see what you're doing to me?

                              TONY
Ride with us, I don't care.

                              PAUL
That's very generous of you, Tony, but I think I'll ride with illicit
couple number two.
    CUT TO:

EXT. DESERT – DAY

*One white Taurus zips past the camera, and after a beat the second zips
past and disappears down the empty desert highway. It is the middle of
nowhere, and they are the only cars on the road.*
    CUT TO:

INT. MEL'S CAR – DAY

TINA *drives,* MEL *sits in the passenger seat reading a roadmap.*

PAUL *sits in the back seat, looking unhappy.*

                              PAUL
He does this to me every eight months. I should be used to it by
now.

                              TINA
What exactly does he do?

                              PAUL
He gets antsy, wanders off with someone else.

                              TINA
I think that's common among certain kinds of married men.

                              PAUL
I'm the rock and he's the flake, so that's life, I guess.

                              TINA
That's what my husband used to say when he was trying to feel
superior to me.

PAUL

Tony's flights of terror from his own life are not about my
superiority –

TINA

It's not terror, it's vitality.

PAUL

I see, is it vitality that's led Mel to leave his wife for you?

MEL
(to Paul)

Would you mind riding in the other car?

CUT TO:

EXT. DESERT – DAY

The two white Tauruses pull over to the side of the desert highway and
stop. PAUL gets out of MEL's car. TONY gets out of the back seat of
NANCY's car, and gets into the front. PAUL gets into the back seat.
MEL's car takes off first.

CUT TO:

INT. NANCY'S CAR – DESERT HIGHWAY – DAY

NANCY drives. TONY sits in the passenger seat, holding a roadmap.
PAUL sits in back with the BABY, holding a bottle in the BABY's mouth.

NANCY

What happened?

TONY turns around to look at PAUL.

TONY

Paul was probably lecturing them.

PAUL

I was asking questions, not lecturing.

TONY

Oh, my God, is that your gun?

PAUL
(*covers his gun*)
You never know when we're going to get beeped for an
emergency.

TONY
You are such a hopeless workaholic.

NANCY
Mel gets like that. Then he can't enjoy anything.

PAUL
If you're afraid to stay committed to our marriage now, what's
going to happen when we have a baby?

TONY
(TONY *turns back to* NANCY)
We were having a conversation, weren't we?

NANCY
We were talking about tenderness.

TONY
You said he's become rough sexually –

NANCY
And impatient.

TONY
What a pity. There's so much to be found in slow tenderness.

PAUL
Like you're never a selfish lover, right?

NANCY
I don't mean to be rude, but I think I'd prefer it if you rode in the
other car.
CUT TO:

EXT. SIDE OF THE DESERT HIGHWAY – DAY

NANCY *sits in her car while* TINA *pulls up next to her and* MEL *leans
out the passenger window to talk to* NANCY.

PAUL *gets out and gets into* MEL*'s car.*

                              MEL

Why can't he ride with you? You're the one who invited them in
the first place.

   NANCY *gets out of her car.*

Where are you going?

                            NANCY

I've got to pee.
   CUT TO:

EXT. DESERT – DAY – WIDER SHOT

*Everyone gets out of the cars and strolls around a bit. Twenty feet
behind them in the desert* NANCY *squats and pees, then comes running
back.*

                            NANCY

OK, let's go. Where are the keys?

                            TONY

You took them with you.

                            NANCY

Fuck.
   CUT TO:

EXT. DESERT – DAY

Everyone is on their hands and knees groping around to find the keys.

                              MEL

Why did you take the keys to pee in the first place?

                            NANCY

I don't know, I wasn't thinking.

                              MEL

How many times have I told you to leave the keys in one place?

                            NANCY

Shut up.
   CUT TO:

EXT. SIDE OF DESERT HIGHWAY — DAY

MEL *and* NANCY *struggle to stuff all the luggage into his trunk.*

EXT. HIGHWAY — DAY

The white Taurus rolls by with the trunk open. A small suitcase falls out and is left behind on the highway. The car stops and backs up for the suitcase.

   CUT TO:

INT. MEL'S CAR — DAY

                    TONY
Nancy was saying you were having some tension around oral sex.

                    MEL
Was she?

                    TONY
Hey, it happens to me, too. A technique I find useful is humming to myself – that can relax me during fellatio.

                    MEL
Humming? That sounds like an amazingly stupid idea to me.

   MEL *looks at* TONY *in the rear view mirror, annoyed.*

                    TINA
Don't you worry a lot about the safety factor in gay sex?

                    PAUL
This may be news to you, but not every gay man is into anal sex. That's where a lot of HIV risk lies.

                    TONY
For example, I'm very anal.
                    (*they all look at him*)
I mean in the sense that I'm compulsively careful and clean about what touches my body, and I'm not into penetration at all –

                    PAUL
To a fault.

MEL

Do we have to talk about this?

NANCY

What are you, homophobic? I want to talk about it.

PAUL

She's testing the risk factor of sex with Tony.

TONY

Don't patronize her, Paul. She knows I came of age in the era of AIDS and even though I'm bisexual, I've been incredibly careful and tested negative three times, most recently seven months back.

CUT TO:

EXT. RANCHO DE ARROYO – DUSK

The charred remains of the B and B sit in the desert. It obviously burned to the ground at least a year ago. The sign post still reads 'RANCHO de ARROYO'.

TONY *stands next to a cactus in the desert, leafing through his travel guide.*

TONY
(*leafing through book*)
We should've sprung for the updated edition.

TINA

Did it ever occur to you to call first?

PAUL

Without spontaneity, the world of B and Bs is fairly meaningless.

TINA

I hope you have a tent, because that's the only way you can be spontaneous in the middle of the desert at this hour.

NANCY

Maybe Mel's parents can suggest a place to stay.

MEL

Great, I'll just show up with about fifty people. 'Hi, I haven't seen you in thirty years, meet my posse, and by the way, my wife invited these gay guys to travel with us, and we're all here without a place to stay.'

> TONY

What does 'gay guy' have to do with this?

> MEL

I didn't mean anything insulting by that.

> TONY

Then why did you say it, 'neurotic guy?'

> TINA

Do you want to file an anti-defamation suit, or do you want to get to the Schlichtings before midnight?

> NANCY

Are they expecting us, or is this another surprise visit?

> TINA

No, I spoke to them, Nancy, I told you that.
CUT TO:

EXT. DESERT HIGHWAY – NIGHT

The white Taurus zips past a lone restaurant/bar called Taco Bite.
CUT TO:

EXT. ROAD – NIGHT

A lone house is lit up in the desert in the distance.

> MEL
> (*voice over*)

God, it's so isolated.
CUT TO:

EXT. RICHARD & MARY SCHLICHTING'S FARMHOUSE – NIGHT

The white Taurus pulls into the dirt drive of a single 1920s, clapboard farmhouse in the middle of nowhere. It is surrounded by some fruit trees, and there is an old barn in the rear and a few little sheds.

The Taurus is parked next to an old pickup truck. MEL *and the others get out of their cars and survey the setting.* NANCY *carries the* BABY *as they walk up the steps of the old-fashioned front porch.*

> MEL

Can't you wait in the car?

> TONY

I'd like to use the bathroom.

The door suddenly opens.

A tall, handsome, blond all-American DAD, *about fifty. He wears a black T-shirt shirt, khakis, and cowboy boots. This is* RICHARD SCHLICHTING. *He smiles warmly as he is joined by a smaller, all-American* MOM, *wearing a fifties-style dress, her brown hair at her shoulders. They look like the perfect parents.*

> MARY

It's so late, we were getting worried.

> RICHARD

I hope my directions were all right.

> MEL

The directions were perfect. This place is really isolated.

> MARY

That's why we love it.

TINA *reaches across* MEL *and* NANCY *to shake* RICHARD*'s hand.*

> TINA

I'm Tina Kalb from the adoption agency. We spoke on the phone.

> RICHARD

That's right.

> MARY

We were so shocked to get your call yesterday.

> RICHARD

I can't believe you saw Fritz Boudreau after all these years. He never got over your mother leaving him for me.

> MARY

Now which one of you is Mel?

                           MEL
That's me.

   MARY *extends her hand and shakes* MEL*'s hand warmly.*

                          MARY
Mary Schlichting.

                      TINA & NANCY
Oh –

                           MEL
So that's how you pronounce it.

                         RICHARD
Nobody gets it right.

   He also shakes MEL*'s hand vigorously.*

                          MARY
This must be your wife.

                           MEL
Yes, this is Nancy.

                         RICHARD
Welcome to our family, Nancy.

                         NANCY
Thank you.

                          TINA
These are our friends, Tony and Paul. They were planning to stay
at Rancho Arroyo.

                          MARY
Oh, dear, poor Rancho Arroyo.

                         RICHARD
Uranium contamination.

                         NANCY
Can you recommend a motel?

                         RICHARD
There's not a decent motel within a hundred miles of here.

                           99

NANCY

Then we'll have to stay here, won't we?

MEL

No – I don't want everyone here.

NANCY
(*steps inside to foyer*)
Look – I'm really tired. I'll just take a shower and lie down.

RICHARD

We put the old bassinet in the room on the top floor.

MARY

Wait – don't you want to eat?

NANCY

I'm not hungry.

MEL

You're not? You're always hungry.

NANCY

Fuck you.

MEL

Whoa.

NANCY

I'm embarrassing you? You just embarrassed me.

MEL

This is not the time or place.

NANCY

You weren't too embarrassed to Indian wrestle with her in San
Diego.

MEL *fumes.*

TONY
(*leaving*)
I'll get the bags. I'd like to lie down, too.

PAUL
(*staying*)

I bet you would.

RICHARD
(*confidentially*)

You're having some problems here.

MEL
(*undertone*)

Yeah, we're having some problems.

RICHARD
(*confidentially*)

Is there some swapping thing going on? Is that what this is?

MEL

No. We're feeling alienated, and these guys are here. That's all.

RICHARD

Who are they? Do you want to talk about it?

MEL

No – I came here to meet you, and that's what I want to do. Who did this?

He approaches a large sculpture of a wiry running man.

RICHARD

That's my work. I have a blacksmith shop in the barn where I do all my sculpture and Mary throws her pots.

CUT TO:

MARY

This is mine. It's a new phase for me – I'm using a new clay.

MEL

Wow. You make your living in the arts.

RICHARD

We try. Sometimes you have to supplement with something else.

They walk into the living room. It is homey, with a stone fireplace, old stuffed chairs and sofas, Native American and Buddhist artifacts. An old clock is ticking.

101

MEL

This environment is so much more creative than the one I grew up in.

MARY

That's so sweet of you to say that.

RICHARD

Listen, Lonnie bagged the quail himself this morning, so let's not let his speciality get cold.

TINA

Terrific. Wild quails.

RICHARD

Quail, you drop the 's.'

MEL

Wait a second. Who's Lonnie?

MARY

Lonnie's our other son.

MEL

I have a brother?

MARY
(whispers)
He's feeling a little threatened about meeting you, so be patient with him.

A door from the kitchen opens and LONNIE *walks in: a nineteen-year-old who looks exactly like* MEL, *but with very long hair, ripped jeans, a cooking apron, and a stud in his right nostril.* MEL *and* LONNIE *look at each other, stunned at the resemblance.*

Lonnie, this is your brother, Mel.

MEL

A pleasure to meet you.

He offers LONNIE *his hand, but* LONNIE *does not shake it. They stand for an awkward moment.*

MARY
(*nervously*)
Why don't we sit down and see what Lonnie's whipped up for us?
CUT TO:

INT. SCHLICHTINGS' KITCHEN – NIGHT

It is a large, fifties-style kitchen. LONNIE *angrily slams a drawer shut, throws a spoon into the sink, and picks up one plate with a small quail and green beans on it.*

LONNIE
(*mutters to himself*)
Ooh, the Special Son is here. Little Cinderella better cook something special for him. Lonnie, make your quail tonight, OK?
CUT TO:

INT. SCHLICHTINGS' DINING ROOM – NIGHT

MEL, TINA, PAUL, MARY *and* RICHARD *are seated at the table, each with a plate of quail in front of them.*

As LONNIE *puts food down in front of* MEL –

MARY
You know what, I think you should sit next to your father, Mel.

MEL
OK.

MEL *and* PAUL *switch seats.*

MARY
My three boys are sitting together.
CUT TO:

INT. UPSTAIRS BEDROOM – NIGHT

A warm, old room filled with pine furniture. The suitcases are on the king-sized bed. NANCY *moves around the room anxiously.* TONY *watches her.*

                    TONY
Are you alright?

                    NANCY
I just need to calm down.

                    TONY
If you need to talk about it –

She puts the BABY *down in the bassinet.*

                    NANCY
I don't feel like talking about it, thank you.

*She opens the door to the adjoining bathroom, turns the light on, and
starts to wash her face at the sink.* TONY *can see her through the
doorway.* TONY *removes his jacket.*

                    TONY
Do you mind if I take a shower?

                    NANCY
No, I don't care.
    CUT TO:

INT. DINING ROOM – NIGHT

People are finishing their meals: MEL, TINA, PAUL, *and* RICHARD,
MARY *and* LONNIE.

                    MEL
Fritz said that you were a scientist, Richard.

                    RICHARD
That's right. I was a chemist for Maple Brothers in the Bay Area
before we came out here.

                    MEL
The aspirin company.

                    RICHARD
That's right, the nasal sprays, the decongestants, all that consumer
crap. I couldn't wait to quit.

MEL

I'm a scientist, too.

RICHARD

No kidding. What field?

MEL

Entymology.

RICHARD

Fantastic. The genetic connection, right?

MARY

Isn't that wonderful? Lonnie never had an interest in science for
some reason.

LONNIE

What's that supposed to mean?

RICHARD

Nothing, come on.

MARY

You just never had an interest, that's all.

MEL

Who knows? I might have had an interest in sculpture if you'd never given me up for adoption.

RICHARD

It's hard to say what might have happened, you know?

MEL

Why did you give me away?

RICHARD

Give you away?

MARY

Thats an interesting way to look at it. Give you away.

RICHARD

It was an opening.

MARY

A release, in a way.

TINA

Fritz Boudreau said you were indisposed – that's why he brought Mel to the agency.

TINA *tinkers with her minitape recorder but can't get it to work.*

MARY

OK – I'm going to tell the story. We were living in San Francisco at the time.

RICHARD

How much detail do we need here?

MARY

I want him to know what happened. Otherwise he'll think we didn't care about him.

RICHARD

Why are you holding on to that?

MARY

You're holding onto it. I want to let it go.

RICHARD

Go ahead and tell him. I'm not holding onto anything.

MARY

(*to* MEL)

You have to understand it was the mid-sixties, OK? We were spending time with a very progressive group of artists, and there was one band at the center of it.

MEL

Which band was it?

LONNIE

Jerry Garcia, blah, blah, blah. I'm so sick of this fucking story.

He gets up with his plate and disappears into the kitchen.

MEL

What happened with Jerry Garcia?

RICHARD

Nothing.

MARY

Nothing happened with Jerry Garcia. But we were sent to prison immediately after you were born.

MEL

You went to prison?

MARY

Don't feel stigmatized by it, honey. It wasn't a serious crime.

INTERCUT TO:

INT. NANCY'S BATHROOM – NIGHT

NANCY *brushes her teeth in the mirror as* TONY *comes in wearing nothing but a towel. She checks him out in the mirror. He has golden skin and a muscular upper body.*

She begins frantically putting her toiletries back into her toilet bag. A glass falls to the floor and breaks. She is growing more nervous.

TONY

What are you doing?

NANCY
(*nervously*)

Nothing. What did I do?

She is practically hyperventilating as she bends to grab the Ajax and a sponge.

TONY

Will you relax? You don't need to do that.

He takes the Ajax from her hand. She immediately backs into the wall and knocks a picture frame to the floor. TONY *stares at her calmly, wearing nothing but a towel around his waist.*

NANCY

There are three Italian prints I have at home that I keep meaning to frame, but should I do it myself or take it to the frame store? I can't seem to make up my mind.

TONY

I usually take them to the framer.

He is calmly staring at her.

Do you want to take a shower?

NANCY

No, you go first.

TONY

I mean together.

She has a burst of nervous laughter.

Your husband's been taking you for granted, don't you think?

The laughter fades, and she stares at his torso. She starts crying.

I didn't mean to upset you.

NANCY
(*crying*)

No, you're right. Let me get my shower cap.

She goes to her suitcase on the bed and rummages through it.

INT. UPSTAIRS BEDROOM – NIGHT

>TONY
>(*follows her*)

I only want you to do this if you feel good about it.

>NANCY
>(*crying*)

I'm going to feel good about it.
>(*she stops crying*)

I just need to find my shower cap.

>*[TONY

You don't need a shower cap.

She finds it and puts it on her head. Then she starts to get undressed, talking nervously as she does.

>NANCY

I can't go to bed with wet hair. My pillow gets soaked and then it gets cold and I flip it over and my hands get cold under the pillow.

>TONY

It sounds very complicated.

He nods as she pulls her blouse off and rifles through a suitcase. She wears a shower cap, her bra, and her pants.

>NANCY

I could swear I packed my shower gel.]

She rushes across the room to another suitcase and starts rifling.

INT. DINING ROOM – NIGHT

>MEL

You made LSD, this is what you're saying, right?

>RICHARD

Let's get one thing straight. There are pharmaceutical executives responsible for all kinds of FDA-approved drugs on the market that have terrible side-effects –

*Cut from completed film

MARY

And they're hanging out at country clubs, they're not in prison.

RICHARD

Acid shouldn't be a felony in the first place.

MARY

It's non-addictive.

RICHARD

It doesn't cause violent crime –

MEL

Did you use acid when you were pregnant with me?

MARY

Oh, that whole thing.

RICHARD

Look. All that stuff about chromosome damage is government propaganda.

MARY
(laughs)
But I *was* relieved that you only had one head when you came out.

RICHARD
(laughs)
A third eye would've been nice. That's a sign of enlightenment.

They laugh with great amusement at this. MEL *does not.*

He doesn't think it's funny.

MARY

You know, identity is just a mental construct.

RICHARD

Have you ever read anything about Tibetan Buddhism?

PAUL *puts his head down and starts moaning audibly.*

TINA

Are you OK, Paul?

He sits up, looking very shaky, and puts his hands out in front of him, humming.

PAUL

Is this a musical table? I'm sorry – was that a strange question?

PAUL *gets up and goes to the living room.*

I feel really sick.

RICHARD
(*shouts, rising, going into the living room*)

Lonnie, get in here right now, goddamn it.

MARY *gets up and follows* PAUL *into living room.* MEL *and* TINA *also follow.*

INT. LIVING ROOM – NIGHT

LONNIE *enters the living room.*

LONNIE

What?

RICHARD

What did you do to his quail?

LONNIE
(*innocently*)

Nothing. Why?

RICHARD

Don't give me that phony innocence. What did you do?

LONNIE

I meant to put it in Mel's dinner, but you moved him.

RICHARD

Of all the selfish, stupid things to do. As if your mother didn't have enough to deal with tonight.

LONNIE

Who *is* he? I mean he shows up, and you like him better because he's more like you than I am.

III

MARY

We would never do that, Lonnie. We love you very much. Even if you were Jeffrey Dahmer we would love you.

RICHARD

I don't know where he gets this insecurity from, it drives me crazy.

MARY

Don't criticize him.

RICHARD

Apologize to Mel and Paul right now.

LONNIE *says nothing.*

RICHARD

Lonnie.

LONNIE
(*looks at* MEL)

I'm sorry.

RICHARD

You're sorry for what?

LONNIE

I'm sorry I put window pane in Mel's quail. And I'm sorry Paul ate it.

TINA

Window pane? What's that?

MEL

It's acid.

MARY

Let's not blow this out of proportion. He'll come down in about ten hours.

TINA

Ten hours?

MEL

I can't believe you still have acid in your house after going to prison for it.

RICHARD

Wait till your son is nineteen and you see if you can control
everything he does.

LONNIE

No way. You can't put that on me.

MARY

Simmer down, you, and take some responsibility for what you've
done.

TINA *lights a cigarette.*

RICHARD

This is a nonsmoking house.

MEL

OK, I think I'll go to bed now.

MARY

I hope we haven't put you off.

MEL

Put off? Why should I be put off?

PAUL
(*sings*)

My secret love in Paris . . .

RICHARD

I hope it isn't because of this – because Mary can talk him down in
an hour.

MARY

I'm an excellent guide.

MEL
(*stands*)

I'm sure you are.

RICHARD

He's just tired.

MARY

That's right. It's a lot to take in.

MEL

It certainly is.

MARY

Open-eyed meditation will help that.

RICHARD

I've got a great book on that.

RICHARD *leaves*.

MEL

It's fine. I'll be fine.

MARY

Sure you don't want dessert?

MEL

No. I'm stuffed.

RICHARD *re-enters with book*.

RICHARD
(*giving him the book*)

Take a look at Chapter Ten.

MEL

Chapter Ten – got it.

MEL *and* TINA *leave*.

INT. UPSTAIRS BEDROOM – NIGHT

TONY

Why can't you just use soap?

NANCY

Soap dries your skin out. Not that I'm one of those women, you know, who obsess about old-looking skin after pregnancy, it's just I happen to be obsessing about it right now.

TONY

Forget the shower. Why risk drying your skin out?

He embraces her from behind. She turns around and touches his chest.

That feels nice.

NANCY

Let me check one more bag.

He follows her, stops her, and they start kissing.
CUT TO:

INT. UPSTAIRS HALL – NIGHT

MEL *and* TINA *come upstairs.*

TINA
(*walking upstairs*)
It's a pro-acid, ex-felon, kind of nonsmoking house.

MEL *goes down the hall.*

MEL

It's an insane house – and where's Nancy? She's up here with
Tony –

TINA

Come on, you need to calm down.

MEL *wanders into a side room.* TINA *follows him.*
CUT TO:

INT. TINA'S BEDROOM – NIGHT

MEL *and* TINA *are sitting next to each other on the twin bed.*

MEL

I can't believe I ruined my marriage to meet these people.

TINA

I'm sorry this is all hitting you at the same time. But after it passes
and things settle down, you can think about starting over.

*They look at each other. They start kissing passionately, running
their hands over each other's bodies.*
CUT TO:

INT. MEL AND NANCY'S UPSTAIRS BEDROOM – NIGHT

                        *[TONY
Do you mind if I look at your armpit?

                        NANCY
My armpit?

                        TONY
It's my favorite part of a woman's body.

                        NANCY
What's attractive about an armpit?

                        TONY
Are you kidding? Lot's of things. Look at this – the definition, the
contours, the depth of the pocket, feel that? So nice.]

INT. TINA'S BEDROOM – NIGHT

                        MEL
                    (breathless)
Wait a minute, maybe we shouldn't rush into this.

*added during filming

You're right. I haven't even finalized my divorce yet.

MEL

No, I could've kissed you just now and felt OK about it, but I didn't. It felt really wrong. Don't take this personally, but with all your nervous energy you kind of remind me of my mother.

She slaps him across the face. They stare at each other.

TINA

I'm sorry. I didn't mean to do that.

MEL

That's all right. You're feeling rejected.

TINA
(*lights a cigarette*)

Why should I feel rejected? You're not an appropriate partner for me. Besides, I don't want to wreck your marriage, you know? I know how painful that is.

MEL

It's not your fault, the marriage is obviously vulnerable at this time.

TINA
(*loudly*)

Every marriage is vulnerable, otherwise being married wouldn't mean anything, would it?

MEL *rises and leaves the room.*
CUT TO:

INT. SCHLICHTINGS' KITCHEN – NIGHT

It is a large, old fashioned Western kitchen with a big old stove. PAUL *sits in a chair in the center of the room, writhing slightly as* MARY *applies a wet towel to* PAUL'*s face and head.* RICHARD *paces, munching on a carrot.*

MARY

Be gentle with yourself.

PAUL

Where's Tony? I want to see Tony.

MARY

Listen to me. Do you have a favorite animal?

PAUL

This is so stupid.

RICHARD

She knows what she's doing. She's an excellent guide.

PAUL

OK, I like dogs.

MARY

What's your favorite dog?

PAUL

St Bernard.

MARY

OK, I want you to picture a big, furry, St Bernard curled up by a fireplace –

PAUL

Can I change my mind?

MARY

It doesn't have to be the perfect dog, Paul.

PAUL

I want to do a Springer Spaniel, how's that?

MARY

OK. A Springer Spaniel.

PAUL

I mean Dalmation.

MARY

Shush.

PAUL

Schnauzer.

MARY

Shut the fuck up – listen to me – relax your neck, goddammit!

RICHARD

Easy, honey.

MARY

He's not listening to me.

RICHARD

Calm down.

MARY

Don't the fuck pet my head! Just give me some wet towels.
  CUT TO:

INT. MEL AND NANCY'S UPSTAIRS BEDROOM – NIGHT

MEL *walks in on* TONY *licking* NANCY*'s armpit.*

*[MEL

Oh, my God!

*Added during filming

119

NANCY

Oh, my God!

MEL

Could we stop all this craziness, huh?

NANCY
(*wiping her armpit*)
Yes. I wasn't even enjoying that.

TONY

You seemed like you were enjoying it.

NANCY

Well, the attention, maybe.

MEL

Okay, alright. Time for you to go.

TONY

You haven't been treating her very well. Do you know that?

MEL

You know what? You've got a lot of nerve, buddy. You come in here, you lick my wife's armpit. I'm going to have that image in my head for the rest of my life; of your tongue in there.

NANCY

You deserve it.]

INT. KITCHEN – NIGHT

RICHARD *restrains* PAUL *in the chair while* MARY *applies a towel to his head.*

PAUL

This is felonious, and I want to make an arrest.

RICHARD

What's he blabbering about?

MARY

He's tripping his brains out. He doesn't know who he is.

RICHARD

Neither do we.

PAUL
(*stands awkwardly*)
I know exactly who I am. I'm Paul Harmon, Bureau of Tobacco, Tobacco, and Tobacco.

He fishes for his badge and finally produces it, then pulls his gun.
RICHARD *and* MARY *are incredulous.*

MARY

Oh, my God.

RICHARD

I told you. It was weird when they called.

MARY

I can't believe they'd do this.

LONNIE

I definitely said not to do it.

RICHARD
(*sharply*)
You just dosed a federal agent. I hope you're proud of yourself.

PAUL

Stay calm and move over to the wall.

LONNIE *suddenly lunges at* PAUL, *knocking him into a wall of pots and pans, which fall to the floor with a great clatter. A large cast iron pan lands on* PAUL's *head, then another. He stands for a moment, dazed, then collapses to the floor.*

INT. MEL AND NANCY'S UPSTAIRS BEDROOM – NIGHT

TONY *is gone.*

NANCY
(*paces angrily*)
I can't follow your fickle little moods all over the place. That has got to change.

MEL

Okay, it will. I promise. Just give me a chance. Let me show you I can be less selfish. I'll show you. You will get concrete results.

NANCY

You have got to earn that back with some consistent behavior, pal.

MEL

I'm sorry I acted this way. I'm sorry I treated you this way. I've got to be out of my mind to risk losing you.

INT. KITCHEN – NIGHT

MARY

Why did you do that, Lonnie?

RICHARD

SHHHH.

They wait.

Nobody upstairs heard it.

MARY *crouches down and puts her head to* PAUL *'s chest.*

MARY

Should we take him to a doctor?

RICHARD

No, let's take him with us as a hostage.

MARY

A hostage? What the hell are you talking about?

RICHARD

I'm not going back to jail, Mary.

MARY

This has to be a mistake. Mel wouldn't do this to us.

RICHARD

Maybe he doesn't know they're doing it. Maybe he's not even our son.

MARY

No, he's definitely our son. I can tell.

RICHARD

If we're lucky, we can make it to Stuart's place in San Miguel de
Allende by tomorrow.

MARY

You want to walk away from a home that took us twenty years to
put together?

RICHARD

Come on. Help me get him outside. Clean out the lab, Lonnie.

RICHARD *bends and picks up* PAUL *by the shoulders.* MARY *picks up
his feet. They carry* PAUL *out the back door.*
CUT TO:

EXT. SCHLICHTINGS' BACKYARD – NIGHT

RICHARD *and* MARY *stagger out the back door carrying* PAUL. MARY
stops and looks out to the far-off road.

MARY

We don't need to take him with us, he'll just be a problem.

RICHARD

What should we do with him?

MARY

We'll put him behind the shed.

They stagger toward the shed, drop PAUL, *and run across the yard to
the house and go inside the back door.*
CUT TO:

INT. KITCHEN/CHEMICAL LAB – NIGHT

LONNIE *puts a key into a door off the kitchen and opens the door revealing
a chemical laboratory with beakers and flasks and other equipment.*

*He closes the door behind him and opens a drawer – it is full of huge
sheets of blotter acid divided into postage stamp-sized squares bearing
Ronald Reagan's face.*

123

He starts rifling reams of the blotter into two big leather portfolios. He also throws in zip-locked bags of chemicals.

CUT TO:

EXT. SCHLICHTINGS' BACKYARD

RICHARD *comes outside and walks over to his old pickup truck.*

LONNIE *comes running from the house with the big portfolios.*

RICHARD
I don't think this is gonna make it to Mexico.

RICHARD *walks up to* MEL*'s white Taurus, which is sitting there with the trunk open. He looks inside the car.*

LONNIE *throws the bag of acid into the open trunk of* MEL*'s white Taurus and closes it quietly. He and his father run back to the house and disappear inside the back door.*
CUT TO:

INT. SCHLICHTINGS' FRONT YARD – NIGHT

A white Taurus rental comes down the driveway and pulls up on the other side of the house. The car doors open and MR *and* MRS COPLIN *get out. She is wearing her sunglasses, as always, and smoking a cigarette. He is stretching his back.*

MR COPLIN
My sciatica is killing me.

MRS COPLIN
We'd have been here an hour ago if you'd listened to me.

MR COPLIN
It took two hours to find out there's no place to get a good sandwich around here.

MRS COPLIN
You can't keep making U-turns in the middle of the highway, Eddie, even if you see what looks like a sandwich place.

MR COPLIN
Let's get this over with, OK?

He walks up to the front porch, but she stops in her tracks on the steps. They now speak in whispers.

Come on, what's the matter?

MRS COPLIN

I can't go in there.

MR COPLIN

Why not?

MRS COPLIN

Look at this house.

MR COPLIN

What's the matter with it?

MRS COPLIN

Its so all-American.

MR COPLIN

What are you talking about?

MRS COPLIN

They could be perfect, quiet parents, and Mel loves them, and we're an embarrassment to him.

MR COPLIN

But he's in trouble, that's why we came.

MRS COPLIN
(embarrassed)

It's possible I overreacted.

MR COPLIN

Now you think you overreacted? We just got off a plane and drove four and a half hours into the desert –

MRS COPLIN

I don't care, I'm not going in there to be rejected in front of his new parents.

MR COPLIN

Yes, you are, you're going in there.

He pulls her onto the porch. She resists him.

125

MRS COPLIN

Let go of me!

She pulls him down the long porch that wraps around the house.
CUT TO:

INT. KITCHEN – NIGHT

MARY *tearfully takes a few mementos from the walls and puts them into a stuffed suitcase she carries.*

*[RICHARD

That's it, we have to go.

He tries to take the bag from her, but she wrestles it from him.

This is attachment, honey.

MARY
(*stuffing the bag*)

It's not attachment.

RICHARD
(*pulls bag away*)

Yes, it is.

She breaks away and gets more stuff.

MARY

It means a lot to me.]

EXT. PORCH – NIGHT

MR COPLIN
(*lets her go*)

You are unbelievable, you know that?

MRS COPLIN

Just get in the car before anyone hears us.

MR COPLIN

I'm starving.

*Cut from completed film

126

MRS COPLIN

We can go back to that taco place.

MR COPLIN

Tacos have cheese in them.

MRS COPLIN

Not all tacos have cheese.

MR COPLIN

Wait, is this our car?

MRS COPLIN

Of course it's our car.

MR COPLIN

Do you remember this truck?

MRS COPLIN

What, do you have early Alzheimers? It's a white rental, and the keys are in it.

They get into MEL*'s white Taurus and leave. After a beat,* RICHARD *and* MARY *run from the back of the house carrying suitcases. They stop in their tracks.*

RICHARD

Where's the car?

They look around. LONNIE *calls to them from the other side of the house.*

LONNIE

It's over here. What's the matter with you?

They run around the back of the house to the other side.

RICHARD

Why did you move it?

RICHARD *throws the suitcases in the trunk.*

LONNIE

I thought you moved it.

RICHARD

Why would I move it?

MARY

Why are we taking this car? I want my old truck.

RICHARD

The truck can't drive eight hundred miles.

MARY

I love that truck.

RICHARD

Just get in.

He pushes her into the Taurus.
CUT TO:

INT. MEL AND NANCY'S UPSTAIRS BEDROOM – NIGHT

They stare at each other. Slow, intimate.

*[NANCY

Are you sure all your doubting is over?

MEL

I'm sorry I took you for granted. I'm sorry I hurt you.

NANCY

I want to go home tomorrow.

MEL

So do I. I want to get out of here.]

They kiss.

INT. COPLINS' TAURUS – NIGHT

They drive for a moment, then pass a Taco Bite restaurant at high speed.

MRS COPLIN

Slow down, that's the place.

*Added during filming

128

MR COPLIN

Why didn't you tell me you saw it?

MRS COPLIN

I did tell you, but you were driving too fast.

He starts to make a U-turn on the two-lane highway.

You can't make U-turns like this, Eddie.

MR COPLIN

Relax, it's the middle of nowhere.

EXT. TACO BITE — NIGHT

The white Taurus makes a U-turn, swerves off the side of the road, and knocks over the big 'Taco Bite' sandwich board in front of the little restaurant; it then swings back into the road as the SCHLICHTINGS' oncoming white Taurus honks and swerves. They hit the brakes, but the two cars collide.
    CUT TO:

INT. COPLINS' TAURUS — NIGHT

MRS COPLIN

What did I just say?

MR COPLIN

He was in my blind spot.

MRS COPLIN

You could fit the State of Wisconsin in your blind spot.
    CUT TO:

INT. SCHLICHTINGS' TAURUS — NIGHT

MARY

It's their fault. They're in the wrong.

RICHARD

It doesn't matter. I don't want some sheriff to come by here. Where's the acid?

LONNIE

It's in the trunk.

RICHARD
(*to* MARY)
Look, if things get tight, why don't you do that spastic colon thing
you do?

MARY

No, I'm not going to do spastic colon.

RICHARD

Something. That thing you did when the cops stopped us in
Albuquerque. You know, that ulcer thing.

MARY

Okay, I'll do reflux.

RICHARD

Alright. That's good.

RICHARD *opens the door of his car and gets out.*
CUT TO:

EXT. ROAD – NIGHT

RICHARD *and* MR COPLIN *survey the damage to their cars.*

MR COPLIN

I'm so sorry.

RICHARD

You can't just make a blind U-turn like that.

MR COPLIN

I've got a sizable blind spot, is my problem.

They survey the damage.

RICHARD

Well I don't see much damage here.

MR COPLIN

No, it looks mostly cosmetic.

RICHARD

It's nothing. Why don't we just forget about it, huh?

MR COPLIN

I don't think we should leave the scene of an accident. I'll call the police from the taco stand.

RICHARD

Well, you can call the police if you want to. But I'll tell you right now – this is your fault here. You make a report and your insurance rates are going to go sky high. It's up to you, but I don't see the point of it.

MR COPLIN

Pearl, he's making sense.

MRS COPLIN

I have never broken the law. I am not going to be irresponsible now.

RICHARD

There's nothing irresponsible about it.

MARY

Absolutely. We're all fine. You can see that we're perfectly okay. I just have this pre-existing medical condition. My ilio secal valve doesn't work as it should and it allows corrosive juices to rise up in to my esophagus. I need to get home so I can lie down and keep my head elevated.

MR COPLIN

Your ilio secal valve?

MARY

It's chronic.

RICHARD

Nice meeting you.

The SCHLICHTINGS *pull out with their dented Taurus.*

MRS COPLIN

Why did you let them get away?

MR COPLIN

We're better off. Who knows what our liability is.

MRS COPLIN
(*reads registration*)

Yes, what exactly is our deductible damage waiver? Oh, my God
. . . the car is registered to Mel.

MR COPLIN

What?

He looks at the registration with her.

MRS COPLIN

Go and see if our luggage is in the trunk.

MR COPLIN *opens the trunk and picks up the big portfolio of acid
and a canister of chemicals.*

MR COPLIN

What the hell is this?

A blue flashing police light falls on him as a sheriff's car pulls up.
CUT TO:

NIGHT TURNS TO DAY OVER THE DESERT
CUT TO:

INT. SCHLICHTINGS' KITCHEN – DAY

TONY

And then what happened?

TINA

I don't know where anybody is. Look at this place, it's a wreck. I
guess they probably –

TONY

I see the place and I'm looking for him and I can't find him.

TINA

They probably took him to the hospital, Tony. He was –

TONY
(*looking out the kitchen window*)
They didn't take him to the hospital. Paul!

He runs out.

TINA
(*looks out window*)
Oh, my God.
CUT TO:

EXT. DESERT – MORNING

PAUL *runs across the desert in his underwear, smeared with mud.*
Enjoying himself.

PAUL
(*running*)
You can't catch the wind!
CUT TO:

INT. SCHLICHTING HOUSE – MEL AND NANCY'S UPSTAIRS
BEDROOM – DAY

MEL *and* NANCY *lie on the bed with the* BABY *in between them.*

*[NANCY
Jerry? 'Jerry Garcia' Jerry?

MEL
Yeah. I mean, it's in the family. It's got a whole history to it.

NANCY
You don't even like the Grateful Dead.

MEL
I never said I don't like them. I just haven't ever listened to that
much of their music. Unless you still like Ethan.

NANCY
This is obviously much more important to you than it is to me,
okay? So you pick the name. I'll just say one thing. I think Jerry is
very pedestrian.

*Added during filming

133

                                    MEL
How about 'Garcia?' Garcia Coplin.

                                  NANCY
Garcia. Garcia Coplin.

                                    MEL
Look, he likes it.

                                  NANCY
I like it too. Garcia.

                                    MEL
Yeah.

   The telephone rings. It continues to ring.

                                  NANCY
Should I get that?

                                    MEL
Sure.

                                  NANCY
Hello, Shit – Shitking – Shly –

                                    MEL
Schleeekting.

                                  NANCY
Schleeektings' residence.]

INT. JAIL CELL ONE – DAY

MRS COPLIN *sits on a bench against the wall in a cell, wearing her sunglasses. She stares straight ahead as she sits between two* TOUGH-LOOKING WOMEN *in their thirties, one with lots of tattoos. They are reaching across* MRS COPLIN, *wrestling over something.*

                        *[MRS COPLIN
                           (shouts)
Alright, that's enough.

   They look at her silently as she holds her hand out.

*Cut from completed film

                                    134

Give it to me.

CHERRY *puts something in* MRS COPLIN*'s hand.*

I'm in charge of the gum now.

                        SUZY
Check her out, Kooz.

                    MRS COPLIN
Your name is Kooz?

                      CHERRY
So what?

MRS COPLIN *makes a face of mild disapproval to herself.*

                    MRS COPLIN
You should change it.
  CUT TO:

INT. JAIL CELL TWO – DAY

MR COPLIN *sits on a bench next to a macho Chicano of uncertain
sexuality with a crew cut who is staring at him.*

MR COPLIN *looks at him then looks away.*

                    MR COPLIN
Would you stop staring at me, please?

  The guy continues to stare.]
  CUT TO:

INT. JAIL CELL ONE – DAY

A young deputy opens the cell door.

                      DEPUTY
You have visitors, Mrs Coplin.

  She gets up and walks out.

                    MRS COPLIN
I'd like a private cell, please.
  CUT TO:

                        135

INT. JAIL – DAY

MEL *and* NANCY *watch as his parents, yelling at the* DEPUTY, *are escorted in.* MEL *holds the* BABY.

                    MRS COPLIN
What kind of trouble are you in?

                    MEL
Us? You're the ones who are in jail.

                    MRS COPLIN
There were drugs in the trunk of your car. Why are there drugs in the trunk of your car?

                    NANCY
How did you get our car?

                    MR COPLIN
We tracked you to the Shit-kings because we thought you were in trouble.

                    MEL
Why did you think we were in trouble?

                    MRS COPLIN
Because of the phone call. The truck and the baby.

                    MEL
I was talking to that evil little dwarf woman at the B and B. We weren't in trouble.

                    MR COPLIN
Your mother, as usual, has overreacted.

                    MRS COPLIN
I did not overreact, Eddie. If I overreacted why am I wearing handcuffs in the middle of a jail?

                    MEL
                 (*to the* DEPUTY)
There's obviously been some misunderstanding, sir. These people are not drug runners. Look at them, they're from New York. They're my parents.

MRS COPLIN

Did you hear that, Eddie? He called us his parents.

MEL

Of course you're my parents. Mom.

MRS COPLIN

Oh, Mel.

She hugs him, catching his hair in her handcuffs.

MEL

Mom. Your chain is pulling my hair.

MRS COPLIN

Sorry, darling.

The door opens and the SHERIFF *appears with a very frazzled-looking* PAUL, *who wears no shirt or pants under his jacket and has mud smeared all over his body and face. His hair is a mess.* TONY *and* TINA *stand on either side of him.*

SHERIFF

Bobby, take these release forms back to the office and get these nice people their car keys. This is all over here. This is a federal agent here, and he just told me the whole story about the Schlytings.

MRS COPLIN

Shit-kings.

MEL

No, Schlictings.

SHERIFF

Well, anyway. It's clear that we have the wrong people.

MEL

That's what I've been trying to tell this guy for the last half hour.

MRS COPLIN

Thank God for this federal agent. And by the way, why are you not wearing pants?

PAUL

I had an experience, that's why.

MRS COPLIN

What do you mean?

PAUL

I resisted at first, and then it evolved, and continues to evolve for
me.

MRS COPLIN

I don't know what the hell he's talking about, but I've got some
jewelry somewhere if you please. Some diamonds and some
turquoise.

SHERIFF

Just let me get those cuffs for you.

CUT TO:

EXT. JAILHOUSE – TINY DESERT TOWN – DAY

An empty street in the tiniest of towns. TINA *helps the* DEPUTY *fix the
camera while she talks to* TONY *and* PAUL.

TINA

We may be able to work out a private adoption with some people I
know in Colorado.

PAUL

How long will that take?

TINA

Usually six months to a year. But if you're willing to wait maybe
you can find a couple of lesbians who would be willing to conceive
and then you could share the baby with them.

TONY

Lesbians are good.

PAUL

I'm not going to do that.

CUT TO: *the* COPLINS, *waiting to have their picture taken, speaking
in confidential tones.*

MRS COPLIN
(*mutters*)
I think these two are homosexuals.

MR COPLIN
(*mutters*)
And they want to adopt a kid? That's so sick.

MRS COPLIN
Can you imagine the neurosis that child will be exposed to?

TINA, PAUL *and* TONY *join the rest of the group for a picture.*

TINA
Okay, here we go. Everyone pull together.

DEPUTY
One, two . . .

FREEZE FRAME *on the group photo.*

CREDITS *start to flash over black.*
CUT TO:

139

INT. MEL AND NANCY'S BEDROOM – NIGHT

NANCY *is tickling* MEL *across the bed again. He's going nuts, until she pins him down and starts kissing him.*
  CUT TO:

INT. COPLINS' BEDROOM – NIGHT

MRS COPLIN *is going down on* MR COPLIN. *He wears nothing. She wears a black bra and underwear. The* BABY *starts crying.*

MR COPLIN
Why do we have to babysit tonight?

MRS COPLIN
Because the kids need some time alone.

MR COPLIN
The kids need some time alone?

MRS COPLIN
God, Eddie, where's your sense of romance?

MRS COPLIN *starts flossing.*

MORE CREDITS.

INT. SCHLICHTINGS' BEDROOM – MEXICO

RICHARD *and* MARY *make love sitting up in a Tibetan tantric position with synchronized breathing and chanting.*

MARY
Shallow . . . shallow . . . deep.

LONNIE *walks in.*

LONNIE
This place sucks. Everybody speaks Spanish.

RICHARD
Did you ever hear of knocking?

LONNIE *starts rifling through their drawers.*

MARY

What are you looking for?

LONNIE

Some weed.

MARY

You find you own weed.

LONNIE

I am totally bored here.

MARY

Honey, it takes time to make new friends. Be patient.

MORE CREDITS.

INT. BEDROOM OF PAUL AND TONY – MICHIGAN – NIGHT OR DAY

A holster hangs on the bedpost or somewhere nearby.

PAUL *and* TONY *make out half nude on the bed while the* BABY *lies next to them.*

*[PAUL

This is making me too nervous.

TONY

It made you nervous when he was in the other room.

PAUL

They both make me nervous.

TONY

I thought this was going to calm you down.

PAUL

So did I.

TONY

Relax – it's OK –

He massages PAUL*'s scalp and kisses his neck while* PAUL *tries to breathe and stares at the ceiling.*

*Cut from completed film

142

MORE CREDITS.

INT. TINA'S APARTMENT– NEW YORK CITY

TINA *sits at a vanity, looking at a mirror, putting makeup on, smoking and talking on a telephone, getting ready to go out.*

>   TINA
>   (*into phone*)
> Yeah, well, we're going to dinner downtown. It's a blind date.
>
> *The doorbell rings.*
> Oh, shit, I gotta go, he's here. Yeah . . . he knows.]

She hangs up. CAMERA *pulls back as she turns to reveal that she's wearing an incredibly tight tube dress and is six to seven months pregnant, showing prominently with swollen breasts. She puts the cigarette out and rushes out of frame, knocking things off her bureau. She exits.*

CUT TO:

INT. MEL AND NANCY'S BEDROOM – NIGHT

CLOSE UP: MEL *and* NANCY*'s faces as they kiss and make love on the bed.*

143

Spanking the Monkey

CREDITS

Costume Designer	Carolyn Greco
Production Designer	Susan Block
Editor	Pamela Martin
Director of Photography	Michael Mayers
Associate Producer	Cheryl Miller Houser
Co-Producer	Jon Resnik
Executive Producers	Stanley F. Buchthal
	Janet Grillo
	David O. Russell

FADE IN — MUSIC — CREDITS INTERCUT WITH THE FOLLOWING:

POV from bus: Ext. Trees wave in breeze in slow motion.
   CUT TO:

EXT. GREYHOUND BUS — DAY

RAY AIBELLI, *eighteen, sits staring out the lower corner of a window as the bus drives through upstate New York. The camera tracks with the window a moment before the bus pulls away and out of frame.*
   CUT TO:

INT. BUS — DAY

RAY *wears a faded Oxford pinstriped shirt. He takes his headphones off, and the music stops. He turns from the window and looks politely toward the camera.*

RAY

Excuse me?
   CUT TO:

ELDERLY WOMAN

I said, would you like another cookie?

RAY

No, thank you.

   She smiles.

ELDERLY WOMAN

What's the matter, don't you like these?

RAY

I'm not that hungry.

ELDERLY WOMAN

They're supposed to be all natural, but you can't believe what they say. Did they give you these up at school?

149

> RAY

No.

> ELDERLY WOMAN

I get tension in my little fingers when there's too much
preservatives. Did you ever get that?
> (*He shakes his head.*)

A summer of home cooking won't be so bad, right? My boys used
to beg for my stroganoff after their first year.

> RAY

I'll only be home a couple of days. I've got a job.

He puts his headphones back on, looks away. She looks away.

> ELDERLY WOMAN

Aren't you the ambitions little SOB.
> (*eating cookies*)

No stroganoff for you.

EXT. BUS – DAY

The side of the bus blows by the camera and disappears down the road.
  CUT TO:

EXT. BUS STOP – DAY

A small town bus depot in Putnam County. RAY *gets off the bus with
his duffel and approaches his father,* TOM AIBELLI, *fifty, who stands
waiting in front of a mint condition cream colored Lincoln Town Car.
He is a fastidious, bald salesman in a suit.*

> RAY

Hey.

RAY*'s smile fades when his father does not smile back. They look at
each other.*
  CUT TO:

INT. TOM'S LINCOLN – DAY

RAY *looks straight ahead as his father drives, tense.*

TOM

She's gonna be fine. That's what counts. It was a perfectly stupid thing to do, but she's depressed and maybe menopausal, and who the hell knows. Anyway, it took twenty minutes for them to do it.

RAY

Do what?

TOM

Pump her stomach.

They drive in tense silence.

Thank God she's all right, because that's the important thing to be grateful for. (*he snaps at a nearby driver*) Hey, why don't you learn how to drive, you fucking moron?

He puts on his blinker, checks the mirror, changes lanes.

It was a tough year. I mean, you left and she was all alone in the house, with me traveling and all, and the hormonal thing and that boring job at the library. Who knows?

He takes the exit for the airport.

Jesus, I almost forgot.

He nervously frisks through his breast pockets and comes up with two bottles of prescription pills in a clear plastic bag.

One's for pain, the other's for tension. Don't let her overdo it.

RAY

What do you mean, for pain?

TOM

For Chrissakes, Raymond, she's got a compound fracture.

RAY

She does?

TOM

Where the hell have you been for the last twenty minutes?

RAY

You said she was depressed and she took pills.

TOM

And I said she fell. Am I talking to myself or what?

He pulls up to the curb at the terminal and gets out. RAY *sits for a moment, then gets out too.*

EXT. LA GUARDIA AIRPORT TERMINAL – DAY

TOM *opens the trunk and takes out his sales case. The trunk is scattered with shrink-wrapped video samples and sales displays.*

TOM

As far as the dog goes, take him on long walks. That's an essential. Good healthy walks twice a day, but your mother's not gonna like that, she'll want you close by. So don't tell her about the walks.

RAY

Don't tell her.

TOM

That's no good. She'll see through that. Tell her you're taking the dog for long walks.

OK, so tell her.

                         TOM

No, scratch that. Tell her I *said* to take the dog on long walks, but say you're not doing it, to hell with me, etcetera, etcetera, OK?

                         RAY

So don't take him on long walks.

                         TOM
                      (*irritated*)

No, damn it, you're not listening. Take him on long walks, and tell her I said to do it, but tell her you're not doing it.

    RAY *looks confused.*

Don't feed him anything but the prescribed food, and that includes the milkbones. I don't spend a fortune on speciality dog food, so he can eat garbage from the table. Here's a reorder form.

    He gives RAY *the form.*

The food should hold out a month.

                         RAY

A month? I can't stay for a month. I'm supposed to be in Washington in two days.

                         TOM
                      (*laughs*)

I don't think you understand what's happening here.

                         RAY

I don't think I do.

                         TOM

I'm sorry, Ray, but you can't go to Washington. I know it meant a lot to you, and we were very, very proud that you got it.

    RAY *looks upset.*

But look. She just got out of the hospital. Who's gonna take care of her?

RAY

There's got to be *some*body.

TOM

But there isn't. It happened at the last minute and this is my biggest trip of the year. We couldn't get anybody.

He pulls out an itinerary and gives it to RAY.

I've got sales conference in Minneapolis, St Paul, then Austin, Los Angeles, Bay Area, Seattle, up to Vancouver, then over to Denver, Chicago, Columbus, Nashville.

RAY

Maybe you don't understand that this was a very hard job to get.

TOM

Of course I understand, and we're very proud.

RAY

The Surgeon General's Office only hires ten interns a year.

TOM *hastily grabs some samples and throws them into the sales case.*

TOM

Raymond, please, it's not the end of the *world*. We all have to give a little something back sometimes, don't we?

RAY *looks at him silently.*

As far as the car goes. You know the rules. You can use the car for emergencies only, and that means what? Emergencies. Not groceries, not movies, not for fun –

TOM *leans into the driver's window and writes down the mileage.*

I'm giving you fifty miles to get home, so the odometer better be this number at the end of the summer. (*He holds the paper up to* RAY.) No, that's not right. You're gonna have to take her to get her crutches and all that, so I better give you a ten-mile bumper here.

He changes the figure on the paper, hands it to RAY.

RAY

What if she's better in a couple of weeks, can I go to Washington then?

TOM *slams the trunk and squints at* RAY.

> TOM
>
> I really wouldn't count on that happening, Ray.

He gives RAY *a toothbrush.*

> RAY
>
> What's this for?

> TOM
>
> The dog. He has a gum condition.

RAY *looks at the toothbrush as* TOM *picks up his sales case.*

Once a week, OK?

He calls over his shoulder as he heads into the terminal.

Be good, and don't worry so much.

He disappears into the terminal and leaves RAY *standing by the car with the toothbrush in his hand.*
CUT TO:

INT. AIBELLI KITCHEN — DAY

CLOSE UP: RAY *spoons dog food from a prescription dog food can into the dog's bowl.*
CUT TO:

A small middle-class ranch house in the quasi-rural part of Putnam County, New York. It is a sweltering June day. RAY *sits down, despondent, at the kitchen table. A fan turns slowly in the window. A dog of indeterminate breed wanders around the kitchen.* RAY *picks up a science magazine and starts reading. Then he turns a radio on, dials back and forth for some music. Turns it off. Sits, bored.*
CUT TO:

INT. DEN — DAY

RAY *sits in the dark, relentlessly flipping channels by remote. The AC drones, muffling all sound.*
CUT TO:

EXT. AIBELLI YARD – DAY

In the humid summer air, RAY *mows the lawn and sweats. The lawn is quite large and in the distance there are other modest split-level homes. The camera follows* RAY *from behind as he cuts the lawn in his shorts and high-top sneakers. Sweat streams down his muscular legs.*

CUT TO:

INT. DEN – DAY

RAY *sits in the dark again, relentlessly flipping channels by remote as his sweat dries.*

CUT TO:

INT. RAY'S ROOM – DAY

It is a narrow, small room. There are large jars with specimens floating in formaldehyde: a fetal pig, a puppy, a kitten, a frog, a snake. On the wall are dissection diagrams labeling the insides of a couple of these animals.

RAY *sits at a word processor with books and clippings spread all around him, typing and reading.*

CUT TO:

INT. KITCHEN – DAY

CLOSE UP: RAY *spoons dog food from a prescription dog food can into a dog dish.*

CUT TO:

CLOSE UP: RAY *makes a vodka tonic in a tall glass, squeezes a lemon into it, and puts it on a small tray.*

He takes the two pill bottles in the plastic bag out, carefully removes one pill from each bottle, and places them on the tray next to the drink. He picks the tray up.

CUT TO:

INT. HALLWAY – DAY

RAY *walks down the hall with the small tray to his mother's bedroom at the end of the hall.*
    CUT TO:

INT. SUSAN'S BEDROOM – DAY

RAY *enters the dim room with the soup and toast on a tray. All the curtains are drawn and an air conditioner blasts. A TV is on at the foot of the double bed, the volume low, playing a PBS documentary on Chinese medicine. His mother lies on top of the covers. The room is dim and depressing. It is an enclosed, self-contained nest.*

SUSAN AIBELLI *has been crying, and her face is still moist with tears. She is a slender, attractive woman of forty-five. There is a light blue fiberglass cast on her left leg. It covers her leg from the foot, past the knee, to halfway up her thigh. She looks drained from nervous exhaustion. She has been wearing the same white shorts and a yellow halter top for too many days, and her hair needs to be washed and combed.*

RAY *brings the tray up to her. Trembling slightly, she picks up the pills and puts them into her dry mouth. Then she slowly picks up the glass.* RAY *sits down on the bed and watches as she drinks enough to swallow the pills, then she puts the glass on the nightstand.*

He sits looking at her. She does not look at him. It is awkward, very quiet except for the quiet hum of the AC and the barely audible words from the TV.

She starts crying. RAY *watches her a moment, then turns to the TV.*

CLOSE UP: TV SCREEN: *Chinese doctors in white operate on a patient, conferring in Chinese while subtitles translate.*
    CUT TO:

SUSAN *sits in bed and cries while* RAY *sits at the end of the bed, watching the TV. He turns and watches her again. He gets up and takes the white bedpan from the side of the bed. He takes it to* SUSAN's *adjoining bathroom and empties it into the toilet, flushes, then rinses it out in the sink.*

He returns the pan to her bedside. Then he takes a box of tissues from the nightstand and holds it in front of her. She takes a tissue and wipes her face, blows her nose. He stands watching her as she continues to cry.

FADE OUT:

FADE IN — EXT. HOUSE — NIGHT

Night has fallen. The lights are on inside the house.

CUT TO:

INT. DEN — NIGHT

RAY *sits in the dark with the dog nearby, restlessly flipping channels by remote.*

CUT TO:

INT. HALLWAY — NIGHT

RAY *walks into the bathroom that is at the opposite end of the hall from his mother's room and closes the door.*

CUT TO:

INT. RAY'S BATHROOM — NIGHT

RAY *pulls his pants down and sits on the toilet, out of frame. He closes his eyes and his hand starts to move in his lap. Suddenly, there is a scratching at the door.* RAY *looks at the door, his hand still moving in his lap.*

RAY
(*shouts*)

Stop that.

CUT TO:

INT. HALLWAY — NIGHT

The dog lies on the floor, scratching at the bathroom door.

CUT TO:

INT. RAY'S BATHROOM – NIGHT

The scratching continues as RAY*'s hand continues to move in his lap while he stares at the door.*

RAY

I said, stop it.

The scratching at the door continues. RAY*'s hand stops and he looks straight ahead and sighs with frustration.*
CUT TO:

EXT. YARD – ANOTHER DAY

RAY *cuts more of the lawn in the hazy heat, walking up and down in long, monotonous rows.*
CUT TO:

EXT. GARDEN – DAY

RAY *waters his mother's tomato and zucchini plants.*
CUT TO:

INT. SMALL LAUNDRY ROOM – DAY

RAY *dumps dirty clothes from the hamper onto the floor. He picks up her white bras and lace panties and puts them into the washer, stuffs too many other clothes on top, jamming them in, and pours soap on top.*
CUT TO:

INT. RAY'S ROOM – DAY

CLOSE UP: *Medical policy journals and articles spread around the word processor.*
CUT TO:

RAY *sits at the word processor, working. He looks tired and rubs his eyes.*
CUT TO:

INT. KITCHEN – DAY

RAY *places a bowl of soup on a tray next to a plate of toast and another*

vodka tonic, puts two pills next to the glass on the tray, and picks it up.
    CUT TO:

INT. HALLWAY – DAY

He walks to his mother's door at the end of the hall and opens it.
    CUT TO:

INT. SUSAN'S BEDROOM – DAY

She sits in bed wearing the same clothes. Her hair looks even dirtier, and her face is tear-streaked and troubled, but she is not crying at the moment. The TV is playing another PBS documentary.

RAY *sits down on the bed with the tray and looks at her as she stares down into the bed. He looks at the TV.*

CLOSE UP: TV SCREEN: *A young, white female physician gives a child a check-up.*

RAY

Maybe you should eat something.

> *She looks at the food. He slowly picks up the spoon and bowl and holds them for her, but she doesn't take them. He dips the spoon into the soup and slowly brings it to her lips. Her mouth doesn't open. He waits patiently. Her mouth opens and he feeds her the spoonful of soup. He gives her another one, slowly. Then she takes the bowl and spoon from him. She slowly dips the spoon in and begins to eat. He watches her take one slow spoonful after another.*
>
> *After a few spoonfuls, she puts the spoon into the bowl. He puts it back on the tray. She takes her pills and swallows them without touching the vodka tonic. Then she takes the bowl from him and starts eating as he watches her.*
>   CUT TO:

INT. SUSAN'S BATHROOM – DAY

RAY *empties a white bedpan into the toilet and flushes.*
    CUT TO:

INT. SUSAN'S BEDROOM – DAY

RAY *watches as* SUSAN *finishes the soup. Then she puts the bowl down and looks at him for the first time.*

> SUSAN

I'd like to not use the bedpan anymore.

> RAY *looks at her.*
> CUT TO:

INT. SUSAN'S ROOM – DAY

RAY *carries* SUSAN *in his arms across the bedroom to the adjoining bathroom.*

INT. SUSAN'S BATHROOM – DAY

RAY *puts her gently down on the toilet seat, then stands straight and leaves, closing the door. He waits outside the bathroom door.*

> CUT TO:

INT. SUSAN'S BEDROOM – DAY

RAY *sits on the bed staring at the bathroom door.* SUSAN *calls to him through the door.*

> SUSAN
> (*off screen*)

OK.

> RAY *gets up, opens the door, and emerges carrying his mother in his arms.*
> CUT TO:

INT. HALLWAY – DAY

RAY *vacuums the hall.*

> CUT TO:

INT. LAUNDRY ROOM – DAY

RAY *folds his mother's underwear into a neat pile.*

> CUT TO:

INT. HALLWAY – DAY

RAY *walks to his bathroom at the end of the hall and closes the door. The dog immediately comes up and lies down to look at the door.*
    CUT TO:

INT. RAY'S BATHROOM – DAY

RAY *sits on the toilet, his hand moving in his lap, while the dog scratches at the door. He turns to the door.*

                                    RAY
Stop that.

    The scratching continues. RAY *gets up and opens the door. He sees the sad-looking dog stare up at him.*

    He lets the dog into the bathroom, then sits down and begins moving his hand in his lap again. But he looks up and the dog is staring at him and he stops, gets up, and turns the dog around so it isn't facing him anymore. He tries to sit down and resume, but the dog turns to look at him.
    CUT TO:

EXT. ROAD – DAY

RAY *walks the dog along the semi-rural road that is sparsely settled with bigger, more opulent split-level homes. It's a distinctly better neighborhood than his own. He sees someone on a bike in a driveway in the distance. He continues to walk.*

Eventually he comes face to face with TONI PECK, *age fifteen, as he passes her driveway which has a distinctive red mailbox reading 'Peck'. She immediately crouches down and pets the dog, giving it her full attention.*

                                    TONI
Don't you go to MIT?

                                    RAY
No.

                                    TONI
Aren't you Ray Aibelli?

                          RAY
Yes.

                          TONI
I know you go to MIT. Why did you say no?

                          RAY
How do you know me?

                          TONI
I go to Central. I'm two years behind you.

                          RAY
I couldn't get out of there fast enough.

                          TONI
I know what you mean.

   He looks at her.

I heard you got a really impressive internship.

                          RAY
Who'd you hear that from?

                         TONI
People.

   She looks at him and smiles. RAY *smiles.*

                          RAY
What people?

                         TONI
Kim Ross. Do you know her?

                          RAY
No.

                         TONI
Well, she knows you.

                          RAY
How?

                         TONI
She just does. It's at the General Surgeon, right?

                          RAY
Surgeon General.

                         TONI
Oh, right.

   They smile.

I hear those are super-competitive.

                          RAY
Are you interested in being pre-med?

                         TONI
I'm strong in the sciences.

                          RAY
                       (*smiles*)
Words that changed my life.

                         TONI
                       (*smiles*)
What do you mean?

                          165

                    RAY

Nothing.

                    TONI

How did you like your first year?

                    RAY

It's not everything it's cracked up to be.

                    TONI

I'd love to get into that school. I got the catalog, so maybe we could go through it sometime.

                    RAY

Maybe.

> *He walks off with the dog. She watches him go.*
> CUT TO:

INT. SUSAN'S BEDROOM – DAY

SUSAN *stands at the edge of the frame, half in and half out, while he holds her up and she takes her clothes off.*

                    SUSAN

Jesus, it hurts to stand.

> *She removes her halter, and then lets her shorts drop to the floor.*

Robe, please.

> *Without looking at her,* RAY *reaches into a closet and gives her the robe. She puts it on while he waits. Then he picks her up and starts toward the bathroom.*

Do you think I'm gaining weight?

                    RAY

No.

                    SUSAN

Are you sure?

> CUT TO:

INT. SUSAN'S BATHROOM – NIGHT

RAY *carries his mother into the bathroom. The white terrycloth robe falls loosely over her breasts. He lifts her over the bathtub, then turns away while she draws the curtains closed and hands him the robe. She turns the water on and showers while holding onto* RAY*'s shoulder through the curtains for balance. His back is turned to the curtains. She showers for a while like this.*

> SUSAN

Shit.

RAY *looks at the salmon-colored vinyl curtain.*

> RAY

What's the matter?

> SUSAN

The soap.

RAY *turns and parts the curtain.*

CLOSE UP: RAY*'s hand reaches in to pick up the soap where it lies at his mother's feet. He stands and hands it to her, catching a glimpse of her thigh, then she yanks the curtain shut. She turns the shower off, and he hands her a towel. She steps out with the towel wrapped*

around her, still leaning on him. He lifts her and starts to carry her out of the bathroom.

> SUSAN

Cream, please.

He leans her over so she can grab a bottle of skin lotion from the sink.
CUT TO:

INT. SUSAN'S BEDROOM – DAY

She sits up in bed combing out her freshly washed hair while RAY *towels off her feet and her fiberglass cast. She wears a fresh pair of shorts and a clean top. She wears glasses.*

She smiles at him.

> SUSAN

The shower was an excellent prescription, Dr Ray.

He offers her a fresh vodka tonic.

Let's skip those for a while.

He looks at her.

They're making me a little too hazy with the Darvocet and the Augmentin and whatever the other one is.

> RAY

OK.

He takes the glass back. She looks at him, still combing out her wet hair.

> SUSAN

I'm sorry you got stuck here for the summer.

She stops and cleans the loose hair from the comb, looks suddenly somber.

I was depressed, and I did a perfectly stupid thing. But that's over now.

She looks at him squarely. They look at each other for an awkward moment, then she looks away and resumes combing her hair.

                              RAY

I'm glad you're feeling better.

                             SUSAN

I owe you a real apology.

   She looks at him again.

We worked hard to get that internship, and it was the perfect extracurricular to get into med school. Exactly the kind of thing I needed to do when I was at your stage.

   He looks at her.

What are you working on now?

                              RAY

Nothing.

                             SUSAN

I hear your little computer keys clicking away.

   He hesitates.

                              RAY

There's an essay contest.

   She looks at him and stops combing her hair.

                             SUSAN

Where?

                              RAY

A magazine at the Surgeon General.

   She smiles broadly.

                             SUSAN

No sense in making the summer a complete loss. What's your topic?

                              RAY

I'd rather not get into it until I'm done.

                             SUSAN

Come on. Just tell me what it's about.

He says nothing.

It's not about transplants, is it?

RAY

No, it's not about transplants.

SUSAN

Because the future, as far as policy that really matters, is all about AIDS.

RAY

I know.

SUSAN

The other areas may be interesting to you, but who wants to end up stuck in a research backwater while the real action passes you by?

RAY

We've gone over this, and I agree.

SUSAN

It happens all the time; it's exactly the kind of mistake I would've made.

RAY

Don't worry, I won't make those mistakes.

She picks up some medical and science journals from the nightstand.

SUSAN

Where'd you walk the dog?

RAY

Over by Trinity Road.

SUSAN

What were you doing way over there?

RAY

Dad said to take him on long walks.

She shakes her head.

SUSAN

He doesn't know what he's talking about.

RAY

It wasn't such a long walk.

SUSAN

Trinity Road sounds long to me.

RAY

That's just what I'll tell Dad. But it really wasn't very long at all.

Pause. She picks up a bottle of lotion and starts to rub moisturizer into her face.

SUSAN

If you're bored, why don't you call some of your friends?

RAY

I don't have any friends around here.

SUSAN

Of course you do. What about Nicky and those guys?

RAY

I don't feel like calling them.

She keeps applying cream to her face.

SUSAN

How about Mara O'Connell?

RAY

Why should I call her?

SUSAN

I thought you liked her.

RAY

Not really.

SUSAN

Didn't you sleep with her last year?

He looks embarrassed.

                              RAY
No. Where'd you get that idea?

                              SUSAN
It's just as well. She was sleazy.

                              RAY
She was not.

                              SUSAN
I thought you didn't like her.

                              RAY
I don't, but that doesn't mean she's sleazy.

                              SUSAN
You could tell she had round heels.

                              RAY
What does that mean?

   She smiles.

                              SUSAN
Why don't you show me that draft now?
   CUT TO:

INT. RAY'S ROOM – NIGHT

He prints the essay on a computer printer.
   CUT TO:

CLOSE UP: *He neatly taps the pages into a stack. He pauses and
thinks. Then he turns and starts to print out another copy.*
   CUT TO:

He picks up the other copy and puts it into a mailing envelope.
   CUT TO:

EXT. GARDEN – DAY

RAY *weeds the garden, sweating profusely.*
   CUT TO:

INT. HALLWAY – DAY

RAY *vacuums the hall while the dog watches.*
  CUT TO:

CLOSE UP: *The dog's mouth as* RAY *struggles to brush the dog's teeth while the dog growls.*
  CUT TO:

INT. SUSAN'S BEDROOM – NIGHT

She sits in bed with her reading glasses on, reading RAY*'s article.*

                         SUSAN
Did you water my garden?

                         RAY
Yes.

                         SUSAN
Including the back row?

                         RAY
Yes.

    He watches her read.

                         SUSAN
I don't know about this.

                         RAY
What?

                         SUSAN
                        (*reads*)
'By insisting that HIV-positive children remain in school, the government can insure they will not be ostracized at the cost of painful and unnecessary psychological trauma.'

                         RAY
What's wrong with that?

                         SUSAN
'Ostracized.'

173

                        RAY

Is it spelled right?

                        SUSAN

'Stigmatized' would be better.

                        RAY

Why?

                        SUSAN

Well, they'd be scarred emotionally, and a stigma is a scar or a
wound.

                        RAY

I think 'ostracized' is fine.

                        SUSAN

Then why did you ask me to read this?

                        RAY

Wait a second.

                        SUSAN

I think you should be a little more open-minded and less defensive
about your work.

                        RAY

I'm not defensive. I think 'ostracized' is fine.

                        SUSAN

Hand me that dictionary, will you?

                        RAY

Why?

                        SUSAN

Just hand it to me.

*He reaches to the bureau and hands her a dictionary. She looks up
'stigma.'*

'Stigma: a mark of disgrace or reproach.' Isn't that what you want
to say?

                        RAY

Maybe. Let me think about it.

SUSAN

You're as stubborn as I used to be. What about this middle section?

He looks at her.

RAY

What about it?

SUSAN

You need some kind of background on disease and federal policy.

RAY

No I don't.

SUSAN

You're cutting corners again.

RAY

I'm not cutting corners.

He sits next to her and takes the essay from her and flips the page to show her.

I thought about it, and I'd rather focus on what's happening right now with the policy.

She looks disapproving as he turns the page.

See, I jump right into what choices are on the table now.

She yanks the essay away and snaps at him.

SUSAN

Do you want to do this right, or do you want to make the same mistakes I did?

She starts writing.

I'm more than happy to help you, but you've got to be less defensive.

He watches as she starts writing in the margins.
CUT TO:

EXT. HOUSE – NIGHT

Night has fallen and the lights are on inside.
  CUT TO:

INT. HALLWAY – NIGHT

The dog lies on the floor and scratches at the bottom of the bathroom door.

After a moment, the door explodes open and RAY *emerges with his pants undone, furious. He raises his hand menacingly at the dog, who cowers away.* RAY *continues down the hall and turns into his room and slams the door shut.*
  CUT TO:

EXT. TRINITY ROAD – ANOTHER DAY

RAY *walks the dog down the road. He comes upon the familiar red Peck mailbox, but there's no sign of* TONI. *He hesitates, then walks on. In a moment, she rides up behind him on a bicycle.*

                    TONI
Looking for me?

  He looks at her.

                    RAY
Just walking the dog.

                    TONI
It looks like you're looking for me. Wanna go for a walk?

  She smiles at him.

                    RAY
I'm already doing that.

                    TONI
I mean to a particular place.
  CUT TO:

EXT. FIELD NEAR A MARSH – DAY

They walk across a big marshy field and approach a dilapidated gazebo in the distance. The dog trails behind.

176

RAY

He's a salesman so he travels all the time.

TONI

Why don't they hire a nurse?

RAY

We don't have as much money as your family does. My father's had a bad couple of years.

Pause.

What's your father do?

TONI

He's a psychiatrist.

RAY

Uh-oh.

TONI

What's uh-oh?

RAY

Psychiatrists' kids are always fucked up.

TONI

They are not.

RAY

Well, Pam Hedden's father's a shrink, and she drove his car into the A & P last year, like all the way back to the meat section.

TONI

I'm not like that.

RAY

Don't underestimate yourself.

TONI

How can you say I'm fucked up when you don't even know me?

RAY

Don't be mad, I'm not saying you're fucked up.

TONI

Then what are you saying?

RAY

Nothing. It's just that she drove his brand new Saab all the way into the A & P and –

TONI

Will you stop it?

He watches as she walks ahead and into the old gazebo, and he follows her inside.

RAY

We can talk about something else if you want.

TONI

I think that would be nice.

RAY

What do you want to talk about?

TONI

MIT.

He watches as she takes out the MIT catalog.

RAY

You think everything will be wonderful when you get into a good school, don't you?

TONI

Why are you so cynical?

RAY

I'm not cynical. You're sunshiny.

TONI

What's that supposed to mean?

RAY

You believe in all the things your parents want.

TONI

You mean I'm naive.

Probably.

TONI

You don't even know me.

RAY

I know your type. I met a lot of people like you at school.

She looks at him a moment, and closes the catalog.

TONI

I don't know why I brought you down here.

RAY

That's a good question. Why did you bring me down here?

TONI

I'm leaving now.

She walks out and leaves him standing there. When she is in the field, he runs after her and grabs the MIT catalog.

RAY

OK, we'll talk about college.

TONI

Forget it.

She tries to take the catalog back, but he holds it away.

RAY

Come on, I'm sorry.

He flips the catalog open, stops and reads.

How about Differential Equations?

TONI

I don't like physics.

He flips the pages, looking for another course.

RAY

No physics, OK. How about Grasses and Pine Forests Under Water Table Stress? I think I'm under water table stress.

She smiles. He looks at his watch.

Oh, my God, I've gotta go.

                              TONI

You've gotta go?

                              RAY

Thanks for bringing me down here.

   She watches him go.
CUT TO:

INT. KITCHEN – NIGHT

RAY *rushes in with the dog and his mother immediately calls to him.*

                         SUSAN
                      (*off screen*)

Your father's on the phone.

   He walks to the kitchen phone and picks it up.

                              RAY

Hello?

                              TOM
                          (*off screen*)

I'm disappointed.

                              RAY

What?

                              TOM

You're not home a week and you leave your mother alone without dinner.

                              RAY

I just walked the dog.

                              TOM
                          (*off screen*)

For three hours.

                              RAY

There's no way it was three hours.

He looks at his watch.
CUT TO:

INT. MOTEL – NIGHT

TOM *sits on the edge of the bed in his shirtsleeves and tie. There are video samples and sales forms in neat piles all over the bed.*

> TOM

All I ask is that you take care of your mother. Is that too hard?

> RAY

But I am taking care of her. You told me to take him on long walks.

> TOM

I told you not to let her know about the long walks. Now she's all over my ass.

> RAY

First you say take him for long walks, then she says don't, then you want me to lie –

> TOM

I don't want to argue, Raymond.

RAY *smacks his hand on the kitchen counter in frustration. There's an uncomfortable pause.*

> (*off screen*)

Guess how many tapes I sold today?

RAY *is silent.*

Take a guess.

> RAY

Half a million.

> TOM

Jesus, nobody could sell half a million. Be realistic.

> RAY
> (*off screen*)

You said to guess.

Use a little sense.

RAY

Why don't you just tell me?

TOM

Come on. Try again.

RAY

A quarter million.

TOM

For God's sake, do you know anything about sales?

RAY

Obviously not.

TOM

I sold eleven thousand. Do you have any idea how many that is for one account?

A NAKED WOMAN, *about forty-five, walks out of the bathroom behind* TOM *and sits on the bed, watching TV with the volume off.* CUT TO:

INT. SUSAN'S ROOM – NIGHT

With nervous urgency, RAY *carries his mother in his arms to her bathroom. She looks irritated.*

SUSAN

The dog doesn't like long walks.

RAY

He loves long walks.

SUSAN

You were away all year, and I walked him and I know. He's not a young dog anymore.

He accidentally smashes her leg with the cast into a lamp, knocking it to the floor.

Ow.

183

RAY

Sorry.

SUSAN

Be careful, goddamnit.

RAY

I said I was sorry.

He accidentally smashes it into the doorway of the bathroom.

SUSAN

What the hell is the matter with you today?

He puts her down on the toilet and withdraws anxiously, closing the door. He waits outside.

RAY
(*to door*)

I don't see why you can't use the bedpan.

SUSAN
(*shouts off screen*)

Because I hate it, and I think I'm entitled to a modicum of dignity, if that's all right with you.

RAY

Shouldn't you have crutches by now?

SUSAN
(*off screen*)

No, I'm still too weak.

RAY

All the literature says you should be mobile as soon as possible.

SUSAN
(*shouts off screen*)

Don't tell me what my body can or can't handle. I know what I need.

He doesn't answer. He waits anxiously. He hears the toilet flush and opens the door.

NOT YET. Wait until I say OK.

> RAY *quickly withdraws and slams the door shut and waits.*

OK.

> RAY *opens the door and emerges with his mother in his arms. He*
> *bangs her leg into the doorway again.*

SUSAN

Jesus.

> *He puts her onto the bed, which is covered with medical journals and*
> *books. A PBS show on medicine plays silently on the TV. She puts*
> *her glasses on and looks at him.*

Who did you see?

> *He picks a journal from the floor and puts it on bed.*

RAY

Nobody.

> *She gives him a 'drop dead' look, then picks up a magazine and then*
> *starts to read.*

SUSAN

I don't care to play charades, thank you.

> *He watches her.*

RAY

A girl.

SUSAN

What girl?

RAY

What difference does it make?

> *He clears dirty dishes. She picks up his essay.*

SUSAN

I'll tell you what difference it makes. I am stuck here in this room,
and I have offered to help you complete an essay so that you can

185

get into a good medical school. I am not doing it so you can play beach blanket bingo.

He looks at her silently as she throws the essay across the room. Pause. She picks up a nail file and starts filing her nails, trying to calm down.

Was it Mara O'Connell?

RAY

For God's sake, will you forget about her?

SUSAN

Then who was it?

RAY

Toni.

SUSAN

Toni who?

RAY

Toni Peck.

SUSAN

Who's she?

RAY

Just a girl. She's got another year at Central.

SUSAN

Jesus.

RAY

What?

SUSAN

She's a little young for you, isn't she?

RAY

I don't know. I didn't ask her to marry me.

SUSAN

Is she pretty?

                              RAY

I don't know.

                             SUSAN

You don't know when you think a girl is pretty?

                              RAY

This is unbelievable.

                             SUSAN

Am I prying?

                              RAY

Yes.

   She drops her magazine to the floor.

                             SUSAN

Let me tell you one thing, Raymond. You can do what you want,
you're a grown man. But you are not to do it under this roof while
I'm here, do you understand?

                              RAY

For God's sake.

   He starts out of the room.

                             SUSAN
                       (*yelling after him*)

Not while this is my house.

   He slams the door as he leaves.

And be sure to use a condom. These are dangerous times.
   CUT TO:

INT. RAY'S BATHROOM – NIGHT

RAY *storms in and slams the door, furious. He turns around and sees the
worried dog sitting there, staring at him.*

                              RAY
                       (*shouts at dog*)

What the hell do you want?

                              187

CUT TO:

INT. KITCHEN – NIGHT

RAY *storms in, goes to the sink for a glass of water, and tries to calm down as he drinks it. After a moment, his mother calls to him from the other end of the house.*

                    SUSAN
                  (*off screen*)
Raymond . . .

  He ignores her. Drinks the water slowly.

Raymond, please.

  He stands at the sink, tense, and fills up the glass again. He drinks the water slowly, then puts the glass down.
  CUT TO:

INT. SUSAN'S BEDROOM – NIGHT

She has her reading glasses on.

                    SUSAN
I'm sorry to bother you again.

                    RAY
What do you want?

                    SUSAN
Did you water my garden?

                    RAY
Is that why you called me?

                    SUSAN
No. I want to apologize.

  She takes her glasses off.

I'm not happy lying around here all day. I'm sorry.

                    RAY
It's OK.

This is driving me crazy.

What is?

The skin on my foot is getting so dry, and I can't reach it. Would you, please?

She holds the cream out to him. He sighs, takes it from her, and sits on the bed. He squeezes some cream onto the foot that is in the fiberglass cast.

Not like that.

Not like what?

Put it in your hands to warm it up first.

He carefully massages the cream in his hands before rubbing it onto the ball of her foot, her heel, and in and around her each toe.

I can never get your father to do things like this for me anymore.

Why not?

You know how he is.

No, I don't know how he is.

First of all, he's never here. When he is, he comes home from work in the crankiest mood.

Why don't you just talk to him about it?

Could you do the other foot?

RAY *squeezes cream into his hands and warms it up. Then he begins to rub it into the foot without the cast.*

RAY

Why don't you just talk to him about it?

SUSAN

He gets mad. He doesn't want to talk. Then I get depressed and I don't want to talk, either.

RAY

Just say, 'Look, this is very important to me. I want to spend some time relaxing with you, but you always come home so tense. I think we could enjoy ourselves more if we gave it a chance.'

He massages the foot, then puts more cream into his hands and moves on to her ankle.

SUSAN

That feels great, honey.

RAY

Why don't you just say that to him?

SUSAN

You can't change people after a certain age, Raymond.

RAY

What's the point of living if you look at it that way?

RAY *squeezes more cream out and massages her calf and her knee.* RAY *is completely absorbed in this task. He squeezes cream onto her thigh. It makes a white squiggle on the tanned skin.*

Whoops.

He scoops it onto his palm and warms it up in his hands. He massages her thigh now.

She sips from her glass, with a clinking of ice, and switches channels by remote, pausing on each station for a little while. As he slowly works his way up to the edge of her white shorts, he becomes flushed, but this is unacknowledged by both of them. The TV seems to cast a veil over what's happening as SUSAN watches it.

CLOSE UP: TV SCREEN: *Enlarged cells move under a microscope.*

RAY *continues to massage her thigh. They both have become sort of glassy-eyed.* SUSAN *speaks in a dreamy, almost drunk voice.*

SUSAN

It itches inside. You never had a cast, did you?

He squirts some cream into the small section of tanned thigh that is exposed between the top of the light blue cast and her white shorts.

RAY *reaches his fingers into the top of the cast, pushing in as far as his hand will go. This goes on for a moment. He is entranced. She stares at the TV, also in a trance.*

CLOSE UP: TV SCREEN: *Cells move under a microscope.*

RAY*'s hand reaches farther down into the cast, as far as it will go. Then he slowly withdraws his hand, stops, and looks at her legs.*

SUSAN

What's the matter?

RAY

Nothing.

He stands up, a little dizzy, and leaves her room.
CUT TO:

INT. HALLWAY – NIGHT

The dog lies on the floor scratching at the bathroom door.
CUT TO:

INT. SHOWER – NIGHT

RAY *stands under the water with his eyes closed, letting it pound the top of his head.*
CUT TO:

INT. RAY'S ROOM – NIGHT

RAY *lies on his bed with wet hair and a wet towel wrapped around his waist, staring at the ceiling in the dim light of a small bedside lamp. He lies for a while, rubbing cream on his chest. His hand drifts down to his crotch, and he starts to masturbate.*

Suddenly there is a banging on the window next to the bed. A flashlight beam shines into the room through the screen. An eighteen-year-old boy speaks in a mock female voice.

NICKY
(off screen, mimicking a girl)

Oh, Raymond. Raymond.

He hears some boys laughing outside. He stands, pulls the towel around himself, and goes to the window. A flashlight is shined in his face.

RAY

Nicky?

RAY *looks through the screen, waiting.*

NICKY
(pops up)

Yes, dear.

192

                        RAY
You scared me.

                        NICKY
What's going on?

                        RAY
Not much. How about you?

                        NICKY
A little of this, a little of that. How was your spring semester?

                        RAY
Not bad. You?

                        NICKY
Ah, too much work, not enough partying. You wanna come out?

                        RAY
I can't.

                        NICKY
Why not?

                        RAY
I'm busy.

                        NICKY
Busy doing what? Spanking the monkey?

   RAY *stands near the window silently.*

Come on. It's so goddamn hot . . . Don't you wanna get out of
the house?

                        RAY
Is Curtis with you?

                        NICKY
Yeah, but he's changed. You don't have to worry about him.

   RAY *stands there, perspiring, then puts his shirt, shorts, and high-tops
   on.*
   CUT TO:

INT. NICKY'S CAR – NIGHT

RAY *is squeezed into the back seat next to* DON *and* CURTIS, *old high school friends. In the front seat are* NICKY *and* JOEL.

> CURTIS
> (*rolling a joint*)
> Yo, Ray, how's college? Are you getting any pussy?

The car bursts into laughter, except for RAY. *Each boy has a beer. A joint is passed around, and the car is full of smoke.* RAY *declines to smoke and passes the joint on.*

> RAY
> What have you guys been up to?

> NICKY
> People's Painters. We'll scrape, prep, and paint your house in two weeks –

> CURTIS
> Or three or four –

> JOEL
> Or five or six –

> DON
> Depending on how hungover we are.

> NICKY
> What about you?

CURTIS *passes* RAY *a joint, which he passes awkwardly to* DON.

> RAY
> Not much.

> CURTIS
> Sounds a little too unambitious for you, Raymond.

> RAY
> I had an internship.

> CURTIS
> That's more like it: an in-tern-ship.

194

                         NICKY

Sounds quite special.

                         CURTIS

Aren't you pre-med, Mr Special?

                          RAY

Yeah.

                         CURTIS

Me, too.

                          RAY

I didn't know that.

                         CURTIS

I may go to a state school, but they got an awesome immunology
lab. I mean, like, going for a Nobel. That level of stuff.

                          JOEL

I'm going for the Nobel Penis Prize.

                          DON

Too late, I already won.
    CUT TO:

EXT. ROAD — DAY

NICKY's *car whips by.*
    CUT TO:

INT. CAR — NIGHT

                         CURTIS

Ray, see if you can do this: first, take a hyperbolic paraboloid and
a cone, and the paraboloid intersects the top of the cone, right?
Now, what's the volume of the cone bounded by the solid?

                         NICKY

Will you shut the fuck up, Curtis?

                         CURTIS

I want to see if he can do it.

NICKY

You know he can do it. The question is, can you do it?

CURTIS

I can do it.

NICKY

Go ahead.

CURTIS

I know you start with the regular coordinates, I mean, that's the first half.

NICKY

Then shut the fuck up.

CURTIS

I can do half.

NICKY

I said shut up.

CURTIS

You shut up.

NICKY *punches* CURTIS *in the arm,* CURTIS *punches him back in the arm.*

Who do you think you are?

They exchange more punches while NICKY *drives and the car veers out of control.* RAY *looks nervous.*

NICKY
(*shouts*)

I said that's enough.

CURTIS *stews.*

What was your internship, Ray?

RAY

Health policy.

NICKY

What happened?

196

                              RAY

My mother had an accident.

                             CURTIS

What kind of accident?

                              RAY

Fell down the basement stairs.

                             NICKY

I hope she's all right.

                             CURTIS

Hate for anything to happen to Mommy, Ray. She's pretty hot, as
mommies go.

                              JOEL
                    (*laughing, with a joint*)
Curtis, you're disgusting.

                             CURTIS

Have you seen his mother?

   They look uncomfortable, glancing from CURTIS *to* RAY.

                             NICKY

Come on, man. Think how Ray feels.

                             CURTIS

How *do* you feel, Ray?

   He says nothing.

                             NICKY

Curtis, will you give it a rest?

                              RAY

Where are we going?

                             NICKY

We found a new place.

                              JOEL

I think you're gonna like it, Ray.
   CUT TO:

                              197

POV – THROUGH WINDSHIELD – NIGHT

Bushes and branches sweep across the windshield as the car drives on a rough dirt road.

CUT TO:

EXT. GORGE – NIGHT

The car is parked in some bushes and the boys walk in the beams of the car's headlights through the bushes. They are guided also by a big flashlight that NICKY *holds in the rear, casting big shadows everywhere.*

About thirty yards from the car is the edge of a one hundred foot sheer drop to the black water below, shrouded in darkness.

> JOEL

Hey, man, give me my lighter.

> DON

It's not your lighter.

> JOEL

It is, too, you dick.

> *He lunges at* DON *and they wrestle in the bushes.* DON *giggles while* JOEL *tries to get the lighter back.* NICKY *walks to the edge of the gorge with* RAY. RAY *looks over and sees the dangerous, rocky drop.* NICKY *throws a rock over.*

> NICKY

I guess you're on the big medicine money track.

> RAY

Do you know what you want to study?

> RAY *keeps looking over the edge while* NICKY *tries to light another joint, repeatedly flicking the lighter.*

> NICKY

I'm gonna major in English Literature.

> RAY *turns away from the gorge and sits next to* NICKY.

> RAY

You wanna teach?

NICKY

Fuck no. You know anything about these new ultrasonic plant
lights?

RAY

No.

NICKY

They're gonna be huge when the ozone layer is gone. This is the
ground floor, like air conditioners fifty years ago.

DON *and* JOEL *continue to wrestle in the bushes.* NICKY *is still trying
to light his joint.*

Hey, will you fuckheads knock it off?

JOEL *stands up with his lighter, glowering at* DON.

JOEL

Asshole.

DON
(*mimics him*)

'Asshole.'

CURTIS *walks up and takes* RAY *to the edge.*

CURTIS

Come here, Ray, I wanna show you something.

RAY *looks over and sees the dangerous rocky drop to a rusting old car
and other debris in the water.*

If you wanna go swimming, there's an open spot of water between
the rusty car and the logs.

RAY
(*smiles*)

Go ahead and try it, Curtis. But I'm not that stupid.

JOEL

We think you're a pussy, Ray, not an idiot. I thought we made that
clear.

Pause. RAY *turns and looks at* JOEL.

199

                              RAY
Fuck you, Joel.

                              BOYS
Oohhhhh.

                              NICKY
That's enough.

                              CURTIS
Mr Valedictorian.

                              JOEL
It's always the same fucking story with you man. You didn't do
acid, you didn't go four-wheeling, you didn't go climbing.

                              CURTIS
And he never got any pussy, either.

                              JOEL
Too scared of the big pussyfish.

                              NICKY
Leave him alone, man.

                              CURTIS
Let him go home to his red hot mama.

   RAY *turns, punches* CURTIS *in the nose, and hurts his hand in the*
   process, immediately recoiling in pain.

                              RAY
                           (*in pain*)
Fuck.

                              CURTIS
                           (*in pain*)
Fuck.

   The others stand there looking at CURTIS *as he holds his bleeding*
   nose and RAY *as he holds his hand. It's an awkward silence.* NICKY
   stands flicking his lighter, trying to light the joint.

> JOEL
> (*laughing nervously*)

I don't fucking believe Ray Aibelli threw a punch.

CURTIS *takes his hand down and looks at* RAY, *fuming. He punches at* RAY's *face, but* RAY *blocks it with both arms, leaving his stomach exposed, which* CURTIS *belts hard.* RAY *falls to the ground, and* CURTIS *commences to pound him until* NICKY *pulls him off.* RAY *lies there a moment with a bloody nose and looks at the blood in his hand. He stands and tilts his head back while* CURTIS *lets his nose bleed.*

> NICKY

Are you OK? He's an asshole, don't let him get to you.

RAY *turns and walks off, alone, into the darkness. They sit in silence for a moment.*

Come on, Ray.

> CURTIS

Busting on that guy is like a bad habit.

> NICKY
> (*walks off*)

You guys said you weren't gonna do this.

> JOEL

What?

> DON

Don't look at me, I was taking a piss.

CUT TO:

INT. LAUNDRY ROOM – DAY

CLOSE UP: RAY *stuffs his mother's underwear on top of other clothes in the washing machine. He touches his side and looks sore.*

CUT TO:

INT. RAY'S BATHROOM – DAY

He lifts up his shirt and examines the bruises on his ribs.

CUT TO:

EXT. YARD – DAY

RAY *lies on his back in the middle of the lawn. It is humid. He is sweating.*

   CUT TO:

CLOSE UP: *Tuna fish and mayo being mixed in a bowl with a fork.*
   CUT TO:

He puts two pills onto the tray next to a salad and an iced tea. Then he pauses and flexes his sore right hand.
   CUT TO:

INT. SUSAN'S BEDROOM – DAY

> RAY

It's time for me to leave. I'm sure there's a way to arrange it so I don't have to stay all summer.

   Pause. The tray with the food is on the bed.

> SUSAN
> (*concerned*)

What happened to your nose?

> RAY

I bumped it playing with the dog.

> SUSAN

You don't play with the dog. Let me look at it.

> RAY

No.

> SUSAN

What's the big rush to leave all of a sudden?

> RAY

I've been here for a while and I'm getting restless. I'm sure you can understand that.

   They look at each other.

> SUSAN

Is it the conversation we had yesterday?

RAY

What conversation?

SUSAN

About having girls in the house.

RAY

We don't have to go into that again.

SUSAN

I want you to know why I said that.

RAY

I don't need to know why. I just want to talk about how –

SUSAN

It's easy to get distracted from your goals at this age. I know because it happened to me.

Pause. She sits forward, and RAY *automatically fluffs her pillows behind her.*

RAY

I said we don't have to go into it.

SUSAN

What do you want me to do?

RAY

Call Aunt Helen.

SUSAN

God have mercy on my soul. Your father won't allow her in the house.

RAY *accidentally knocks over a glass of water on the nightstand. He starts to clean it up.*

RAY

We don't have to tell him.

SUSAN

That would be hard to get away with.

RAY

How can you keep track of his stupid rules?

SUSAN

Don't talk about him that way.

RAY

It's true.

SUSAN

Well, he wasn't always such a crank.

RAY

I find that hard to believe.

SUSAN

When I met him, he had a convertible and an apartment in New York where he threw lots of parties. He made more money than anyone else I knew.

RAY

Big, deal. If you'd gone to medical school, you'd be earning a lot more than he does, wouldn't you?

SUSAN

Don't start this again.

RAY

It's true.

SUSAN

Raymond.

She puts her glasses on and picks up his essay.

RAY

You could always go back to school.

SUSAN

I don't have your discipline.

He takes the essay away from her.

RAY

You read more than I do.

SUSAN

I can't do it.

RAY

Why not?

She looks at him spitefully.

SUSAN

That was the deal.

RAY

What deal?

SUSAN

Your father didn't want to have children. OK?

RAY

What does that have to do with anything?

SUSAN

A lot.

RAY *lets this sink in.*

RAY

He didn't want to have children?

SUSAN

He doesn't feel that way anymore. I'd like to take my shower now,
if you don't mind.

CUT TO:

INT. SUSAN'S BATHROOM – DAY

RAY *stands with his back to the shower curtain while his mother holds
onto his shoulder and showers.*

SUSAN

If it's that important to you, I'll call Helen, but there's no
guarantee she'll be available. Give me the washcloth from the sink.

RAY *looks at the washcloth, then slowly picks it up. He turns and
hands it to her. She hands it back to him wet and soapy.*

RAY

What do you want me to do with this?

205

SUSAN

Wash my back.

RAY *holds the soapy, dripping washcloth without doing anything at first. Then, he reaches in and washes her back. His eyes drift down her body.*

RAY

Is that a birthmark?

SUSAN

Raymond.

RAY

Don't blame me if this set up doesn't give you any privacy.

He tilts his head to sneak another look.

It's shaped sort of like a little shopping cart, isn't it?

SUSAN

Would you give me the soap, please?

He hands her the soap while continuing to hold her up.

You never were inhibited when you were little, and that's not true of every child, you know. Did I ever tell you that story about New Year's Eve when you were about three?

RAY

I don't think so.

RAY *kneels down, holding her hand to steady her, and washes the leg without the cast.*

SUSAN

It was when we drove cross country. You were always reaching into your pants. You couldn't keep your hands out of there. I didn't mind, but it drove your father crazy. We were eating in this restaurant in Salt Lake and all of a sudden you shouted: 'There's a piece of toilet paper on my penis!'

She laughs, then turns the shower off and suddenly slips and falls into the curtain, ripping it from the rings. He catches her.

RAY

Are you OK?

He stands her up and steadies her. She wraps herself in the torn shower curtain.

SUSAN

How do you like my toga?

She laughs, he smiles. They hear the phone ringing. Susan's answering machine picks up: 'You've reached the Aibelli residence, please leave us a message BEEP.'
CUT TO:

INT. SUSAN'S BEDROOM – DAY

RAY *struggles to get* SUSAN *through the bathroom door while the answering machine plays.*

DR WILSON
(*on machine*)
This is Doctor Joyce Wilson at the Surgeon General's office.

RAY *carries* SUSAN *to the bed.*

We were so disappointed Raymond couldn't join us this summer, and when we got his essay on federal policy for children with AIDS, we were super impressed –

SUSAN

What is she talking about?

DR WILSON
(*on machine*)
I've talked to our budget office and –

SUSAN
(*picks up phone*)
He hasn't finished that essay, we're still working on it.

DR WILSON
(*off screen*)

Mrs Aibelli?

                              SUSAN
Yes.

                            DR WILSON
                           (*off screen*)
The essay sure looked finished to me, and very well written, I
might add.

   SUSAN *looks at* RAY.

I hope your recovery is going well.

                              SUSAN
It's fine.

                            DR WILSON
                           (*off screen*)
Good. Because I've talked to our budget office, and they're willing
to double Raymond's disbursement so you could hire a nurse.
How does that sound?

                              SUSAN
I'll have to discuss it with Raymond, I mean my husband.

                            DR WILSON
                           (*off screen*)
We'd love him to come down this weekend.

                              SUSAN
This weekend?
   CUT TO:

INT. SURGEON GENERAL'S OFFICE – NIGHT

DR JOYCE WILSON, *a woman about* SUSAN*'s age, sits in a large office.
She wears a suit, and she speaks into the phone.*

                            DR WILSON
I know it's short notice, but we're having a conference and it
would be an ideal opportunity for Raymond to meet everyone.

                              SUSAN
I'll have to get back to you.

DR WILSON

Of course. I look forward to hearing from you.

SUSAN *hangs up the phone, in a state of shock.*

SUSAN

You sent them the essay?

RAY

I'm sorry.

SUSAN

You didn't have to let me keep working on it like some idiot when they already had it.

RAY

You were so stubborn about working on it, I thought you enjoyed it.

SUSAN

Sure, indulge your poor bedridden mother.

RAY

What did they say?

SUSAN

They're giving you more money so we can hire a nurse. They want you to go down this weekend.

RAY *explodes into a smile and jumps to his feet.*

RAY

I guess they liked the essay quite a bit.

SUSAN

I'm not surprised. You're a good writer.

RAY

This is fantastic, isn't it? Just when you think there's no solution.

SUSAN

You got what you wanted. I'm happy for you.

RAY

It's pretty short notice to get a nurse by this weekend, isn't it?
(*he thinks*)

I guess we could get Helen to fill in until we get one, right?

He suddenly notices how sad she looks.

It won't be that bad. You get your crutches soon. You're gonna be more mobile. Maybe you could go back to work early.

She smiles.

SUSAN

Maybe.

RAY

Hey, I know. You could take the train down and visit me. I bet you'd like to meet the editors of some of these journals, wouldn't you?

SUSAN

Yes. That would be nice.

She smiles wanly.

RAY

I'll get these dirty dishes out of here for you, then I guess I better start packing.

SUSAN

Yep.

RAY

Should I call Aunt Helen?

SUSAN
(*dully*)

No, I'll call her.

He heads out with the tray. She stares straight ahead.

RAY
(*on his way out*)

Do you need anything?

SUSAN

Vodka tonic.

RAY
(leaves)

You got it.

> *He closes the door, leaving her alone in her big bed with the TV screen flickering silently as her smile fades.*
> CUT TO:

INT. RAY'S ROOM – DAY

He packs a big suitcase.
> CUT TO:

He packs his computer.
> CUT TO:

CLOSE UP: *The dog growls as* RAY *forcibly brushes the dog's teeth.*
> CUT TO:

RAY *sits on his bed looking nervous with his packed bags nearby. He looks at his watch. Thinks.*
> CUT TO:

INT. FRONT DOOR OF TONI'S HOUSE – DAY

The door opens and DR PECK, *a distinguished looking man with horn-rimmed glasses, looks down at* RAY, *who holds a bag of groceries. The dog paces in the background.*

DR PECK

Can I help you?

RAY

Hi, I'm Ray Aibelli.

> DR PECK *scowls down at* RAY *skeptically for a moment while* RAY *looks back hopefully, a little intimidated.*

Is Toni here?

DR PECK

Is she expecting you?

RAY

I don't think so.

211

DR PECK's *response is to stare at* RAY *another moment, then withdraw into the house and close the door.* RAY *waits nervously. After a moment, the door opens again and* TONI *appears and looks at* RAY.

TONI

I didn't think I'd be seeing you again.

RAY

I can go to Washington. They're giving me more money, I can go.

She smiles slowly.

TONI

The cynic is psyched.

CUT TO:

EXT. MARSHY FIELD WITH GAZEBO IN DISTANCE – DUSK

RAY *and* TONI *head toward the gazebo.* RAY *is bursting with energy, walking backwards, sideways, around* TONI *as she walks.*

TONI

So what do they do down there?

RAY

Lots of policy stuff.

TONI

Like what?

RAY

Substance abuse, organ transplants, and underage drinking. Then there's smoking, comprehensive care for families with HIV, and child health, which breaks down to childhood injury, childhood immunization. Then women, adolescents, and children with AIDS.

She laughs at the litany.

TONI

Which one do you like to work on?

RAY

Which one do I like?

TONI

What's your main interest?

RAY

I have no idea.

TONI

That's weird.

RAY

Why is it weird?

TONI

I just thought you'd have a real passion for something.

RAY

I think I like organ transplants.

TONI

Is that what you wrote about?

RAY

No, I wrote about children with AIDS.

TONI

How come?

RAY

Because that's where people say the future is.
  CUT TO:

INT. GAZEBO – NIGHT

RAY *and* TONI *make out in a very wooden and stiff fashion. The kisses are very dry and stiff. They stop and start several times. At one point, she pulls out her retainer. This goes on for a moment, before* TONI *pulls back.*

TONI

What's wrong?

RAY

Nothing.

  She flips her hair back.

TONI

Are you sure?

RAY

I don't want to do anything you're not comfortable with.

Pause.

TONI

I think I'm pretty comfortable with this.

RAY

Your lips aren't moving.

TONI

They're not?

RAY

No.

He looks at her. He starts kissing her again. It remains wooden, except this time he carefully, dispassionately runs his hand over her breasts on the outside of her shirt. He stops kissing her and looks at her breasts as if they were specimens, touching them in this way.

TONI

Can I ask you something?

RAY

What?

TONI

Are you attracted to me?

RAY

Will you relax?

TONI

I am relaxed.

RAY

Then stop talking.

He kisses her again in the same careful way. She pulls back at the end of the kiss. He is exasperated.

214

TONI

Do you have a girlfriend at school or something?

RAY
(*exasperated*)

No. Why?

TONI

Because I think you're holding back for some reason.

RAY

I'm not.

TONI

Are you gay?

RAY

What are you talking about?

TONI

It's totally cool with me, because there's no judging sexual preference.

RAY

What?

TONI

I just want you to know it's not an issue with me.

RAY

Look. What are you so nervous about?

TONI
(*nervous*)

I'm not nervous, I'm just saying, I've read a lot about gender politics and I'm totally comfortable with whatever. I'm not nervous.

RAY

Will you shut up?

TONI

Don't tell me to shut up.

RAY

I'm sorry, but you just keep talking.

They sit for a moment. Then he leans in and starts kissing her much harder. He starts biting her neck.
CUT TO:

The dog has torn open the bag of groceries on the grass and is tearing into a cottage cheese container.
CUT TO:

RAY *has gone to the other extreme and is practically ravaging* TONI, *kissing her very hard and fondling her all over. Her blouse is open. She looks scared as he continues ravenously.*

TONI

Wait.

She watches him, scared, uncomfortable. RAY *starts to pull* TONI*'s pants open.*

Wait.

He doesn't stop. She pulls away, to the other side of the gazebo. He pursues her. She pulls away again.

What are you doing?

He finally stops, out of breath, looking at the floor. She looks at him, also out of breath. She starts to button her blouse.

> RAY
> (*out of breath*)

What's the matter now?

> TONI

You don't have to rape me to prove something, my God.

> RAY

I'm not.

He stands up and tucks his shirt in. She starts crying.

I knew we shouldn't have done this. You're way too young.
  CUT TO:

EXT. ROAD — NIGHT

RAY *and* TONI *walk silently down the road, looking straight ahead. They come to her driveway and stop. He is holding the shredded remains of the bag of groceries. The dog follows with cottage cheese all over his face.* RAY *and* TONI *stand silently at her driveway. They stand there an awkward moment. She runs down her driveway. He watches her go.*
  CUT TO:

INT. KITCHEN — NIGHT

CLOSE UP: *A large knife chops a pineapple in half.*
  CUT TO:

AUNT HELEN, *an imposing woman, sixty-five, with intense eyes. She turns from a cutting board where she is chopping up a pineapple.*

> AUNT HELEN

Farmer's cheese is very good for the bones, loaded with calcium to hasten ossification. Pineapple gives you acid to aid digestion. But you already know things like that, don't you, Doctor Raymond?

He watches her cut the pineapple. There is a plate of farmer's cheese next to the cutting board.

217

AUNT HELEN

I'd forgotten what the inside of this house looks like. They haven't done much with it, have they? You probably have no idea what your own cousins are up to, do you?

RAY

Not really.

AUNT HELEN

Richard is a bond trader. He just bought a second home in Rhode Island. Cathy is a chiropractor in Rochester and she lives with Howard. He teaches yoga. You should visit them.

RAY

I don't get up to Rochester very often.

AUNT HELEN

You could always call. Just pick up the phone.

RAY

We were never very close.

AUNT HELEN

Family is our greatest asset; you'll find that out as you get older.
CUT TO:

INT. HALL — NIGHT

RAY *walks down the hall with a drink and pills on a tray.*
CUT TO:

INT. SUSAN'S BEDROOM — NIGHT

RAY *walks in and* SUSAN *sits unhappily in bed. He hands her the vodka tonic, which she takes and does not sip. He watches her a moment, though she does not look at him.*

RAY

I got the groceries, and I watered the garden, and I changed the shower curtain. Helen's all set with the house and the dog. She has a list of nurses she's going to call. So everything's under control.

218

SUSAN

Good. Close the door.

RAY

Why?

SUSAN

I have to tell you something.

RAY

Why do I have to close the door?

SUSAN

Fine, leave it open.

He goes over, closes the door, comes back and looks at her.

I got a phone call from your little friend's father.

RAY

Who?

SUSAN

Dr Peck. That's his name isn't it?

He is shocked.

RAY

Toni's father called?

Pause. RAY looks tense. She does not look at RAY when she talks, but draws boxes around her crossword puzzle.

SUSAN

He said you got too rough with his daughter.

He looks deeply embarrassed. She pauses.

He wanted to know if you'd ever been to a shrink . . . There was also some ridiculous comment about the state of your sexual identity.

Pause.

We don't have to talk about it if you don't want to, but it might be a good idea.

Long pause.

                    RAY

I can't believe she talked to her father.

                   SUSAN

What happened?

                    RAY

First, she was nervous and stiff, so I went slow. Then she
complained, so I went faster, and she said I was raping her.

                   SUSAN

What exactly did you do to her?

> AUNT HELEN *comes in with a tray of cheese and pineapple. They
> look up at her as she puts the tray on the bed.*

                 AUNT HELEN

Ready for more calcium?

                   SUSAN

No more cheese, Helen.

                 AUNT HELEN

That's not what your bones would say.

                   SUSAN

We're having a private conversation.

                 AUNT HELEN

I can take a hint.
                    (puts tray down, spills)
Oh, look what I've done.

                   SUSAN

That's OK, just leave us, please.

                 AUNT HELEN

Raymond's off to the train at six a.m., is that correct?

                   SUSAN

Fine.

                 AUNT HELEN

Tom doesn't think I'm a good driver but I've never had an

accident in thirty years. Once someone bumped into me at a stop sign, but that wasn't my fault, and Tom brings it up every single time –

SUSAN

Helen!

AUNT HELEN

No need to shout.

She leaves, slamming the door.

SUSAN
(*mimics* AUNT HELEN)
'Once someone bumped into me at a stop sign'.

RAY *sits sullenly on the bed.*

RAY

I can't believe that bitch talked to her father.

SUSAN

Hey.

RAY

Why did she do it?

SUSAN

I told you to watch who you fool around with, or there would be problems.

RAY

Why is it so goddamn complicated?

SUSAN

It's not exactly a physics problem.

RAY

It may as well be.

SUSAN

Some girls don't know what they want.

SUSAN *takes two pills and gulps from a fresh vodka tonic. She puts the glass down.*

There are times for everybody when sex is awkward. You just can't force yourself on someone.

RAY

I didn't.

SUSAN

Apparently she thinks you did.

RAY

But I didn't.

SUSAN

Then why does she think you did?

RAY

Look –

He sits next to his mother.

We were sitting like this and it got real quiet and she was staring at me – so stare at me –

SUSAN *stares at him at close range.*

So she wants me to kiss her, right? And I did. Her lips weren't moving at all.

SUSAN

What do you mean, not moving at all?

RAY

Like this –

He puts his mouth to her cheek, not moving his lips, then he puts his mouth to her mouth, not moving his lips.

OK, so I was real careful. But then she asks *me* what's wrong and am I attracted to her and am I GAY, for God's sake. So I kissed her harder. I was touching her around here, you know, and a little lower –

He rubs her arm roughly.

SUSAN

Like what? That's pretty hard.

222

RAY
No, it's not.

                                SUSAN
                        (*mimics his rubbing*)
This is hard, isn't it? You've gotta be gentle. You know how to be
gentle.

   She strokes his arm.

Feel this? That's how you touch her. Feel her skin, smell her hair.

   They touch hands and arms for a while.

I don't think she should have talked to her father, or called you
names.
                        (*pause, touching*)
You better get to sleep, you've got an early train.

   He looks at her, then leaves.
   CUT TO:

EMPTY LIVING ROOM — NIGHT

EMPTY KITCHEN — NIGHT

EMPTY RAY'S BATHROOM — NIGHT

EMPTY HALLWAY — NIGHT
   CUT TO:

INT. RAY'S ROOM — NIGHT

*He lies on top of his sheets in his boxers, tossing and turning. He cannot
sleep. He gets up, puts his shorts and a T-shirt on, and leaves.*
   CUT TO:

INT. HALLWAY — NIGHT

RAY *looks into the spare room and sees* AUNT HELEN *sleeping. He
continues down the hall to his mother's room. The door is open a crack.
Inside it is dark, except for a blue TV glow. He pushes the door open
and she looks up at him, then looks at the clock. She wears her robe.*

223

INT. SUSAN'S BEDROOM – NIGHT

                              SUSAN
Are you still up?

                              RAY
I can't sleep.

                              SUSAN
You're just nervous about your trip.

   He stands there. She looks at him.
   CUT TO:

INT. KITCHEN – NIGHT

RAY *cracks open an ice tray and clinks the cubes into two tall glasses.
He pours a lot of vodka in each glass.*
   CUT TO:

INT. SUSAN'S ROOM – NIGHT

RAY *and* SUSAN *sit side by side watching a medical show. Their drinks
are nearly empty.* RAY *looks sleepy.* SUSAN *picks up a piece of cheese
and eats it.*

                              SUSAN
She keeps bringing me this goddamned cheese, and I keep eating
it.

   RAY *picks up a hunk of farmer's cheese and flings it across the room.
   She smiles and does the same thing. They fling all the cheese and
   pineapple against the wall, giggling nervously. When it's all gone,*
   RAY *looks at the mess.*

   She puts her drink down, then tries to turn over, with difficulty. RAY
   finally helps her roll onto her stomach.

                              RAY
Are you OK?

                              SUSAN
Another cramp.

RAY

Where?

SUSAN

My hip.

He looks at her as she lies on her stomach, then reaches over and massages her left hip.

Other hip.

He massages her right hip. He does this for a moment, looking at her bottom and the backs of her legs.

After a moment, he stops and resumes watching TV.

Thanks.

He notices the lotion on the nightstand. He reaches for it and rubs some cream into his hands. The he starts to massage the backs of her thighs. He does this for a while, working higher under her shorts toward her buttocks. He works the inside of her thighs. His face is intent on this.

SUSAN's hand reaches down to her robe and pulls it up slightly. She gives him a dark look over her shoulder, inviting. He moves his hand up to her crotch, then leans over her, lowering himself.
FADE OUT:

FADE IN — INT. KITCHEN — DAY

CLOSE UP: *Two white eggs boil in a blue pot.*
CUT TO:

WIDER SHOT: AUNT HELEN *prepares a breakfast tray at the counter.*
CUT TO:

INT. SUSAN'S ROOM — DAY

The camera pulls back and reveals RAY sprawled across the bed, asleep, and his mother facing the other way, nude, also sleeping. RAY's boxer shorts are on.

He slowly wakes up. He looks very groggy and hungover. He sits on the side of the bed and holds his head in his hands. SUSAN rolls onto her

225

back and stretches, also looking hungover, and reaches for a nearly empty glass. She drinks the dregs, leaving a dried up lime. They sit in depressed silence, SUSAN *starts to cough and it turns into a coughing fit that goes on for an uncomfortable length.*

> SUSAN
> (*dryly*)

Could I have some water?

RAY *reaches across her and takes the glass. He gets up and goes to the bathroom. We hear the water run while* SUSAN *sits up in bed and covers herself with a sheet.*

RAY *returns, hands her the water, and sits down with disgust. There's a sharp knock on the door.*

> AUNT HELEN
> (*off screen*)

Raymond missed his train.

RAY *jumps up and grabs his clothes from the floor.*

> SUSAN
> (*calls to the closed door*)

Just a minute.

RAY *pulls up the blinds and tries to open the first floor bedroom window, but it is stuck.*

> AUNT HELEN
> (*off screen*)

His bed's empty, but his bag is still here.

> SUSAN

I'm sure he's around somewhere.

> AUNT HELEN
> (*off screen*)

You can't expect me to get in to help you with a locked door. How did you lock this door, anyway?

RAY *bangs at the window and gets it to open.*
CUT TO:

EXT. YARD – DAY

He climbs out, dropping to the grass outside.

RAY *stands in the yard on the side of the house in his boxer shorts, dazed. He walks quickly around the house, ducking past the windows.*
CUT TO:

AUNT HELEN
(*at bedroom door*)
I should think you would trust me enough to not lock the door.

SUSAN
It's not a matter of trust, Helen, don't take it that way.
CUT TO:

EXT. YARD – DAY

RAY *runs to the driveway in his boxers, carrying his clothes and –*

POSTMAN
Good morning.

RAY *turns, startled. The* POSTMAN *walks up to him and gives him a pack of mail and a package.*

Is everything all right?

RAY
Yeah.

The POSTMAN *looks deadpan at* RAY*'s appearance, turns and leaves* RAY *standing there with the mail.*
CUT TO:

INT. HALLWAY – DAY

RAY *opens a closet and pulls out a wire hanger. He then walks down the hall to where his old aunt holds a tray outside* SUSAN*'s room.*

AUNT HELEN
Where in the world have you been?

RAY
Out for a walk.

Without your shoes?

> RAY *untwists the wire hanger and puts the straight end into a small hole in the knob and pops the door open.*

What is that cheese doing all over the floor?

> *They watch her silently as she puts the tray on the bed and cleans up the mess on the floor.*

I swear this is the most disorganized house in all of America.

> *She picks the tray up and puts it on the bed. The phone starts ringing. Nobody moves. It rings four times.*

Isn't anyone going to get the phone?

> *They watch it.* SUSAN *finally reaches over slowly and picks it up.*

SUSAN

Hello?

TOM
(*off screen*)
What's going on? Nobody answers the damn phone.

SUSAN
Tom, what a surprise to hear from you.

TOM
Don't start, Susan. I'm in a real jam here. Where the hell is Ray?

SUSAN
He's here.

TOM
Is he staying in?

> *She looks at* RAY *for a moment.*

SUSAN
That's for sure.

TOM
Good. Put him on.

She holds the phone out to RAY, *who looks at it, frightened, and shakes his head. She keeps holding it out to him until he finally takes it.*

> RAY
> *(into phone)*

Hello?

> TOM

What the hell's going on? Nobody answers the damn phone.

> RAY

Sorry. I was outside.
>   CUT TO:

INT. MOTEL – DAY

It's a different motel room. TOM *anxiously fumbles through his samples and his briefcase, late for a meeting. He has a different shirt and tie on. Behind him, a different woman of forty-six, a little heavy with big breasts, is in a slip and a bra, combing out her hair. She approaches with a glass of OJ and he waves her off, irritated.*

> TOM

I'm in real trouble. I need some very important samples.

> RAY
> *(off screen)*

Where are they?

> TOM

Go in my office and look on the floor, behind the desk. Sample tapes called 'Exercise for Executives.'
>   CUT TO:

INT. SUSAN'S BEDROOM – DAY

RAY *puts the phone down and looks at his mother, who looks back at him. Then he gets up and leaves the bedroom.*

AUNT HELEN *sits in a chair watching* SUSAN *talk on the phone.*

> SUSAN

Why don't you come home and get the samples yourself?

TOM

I'm in danger of losing a major account, Susan.

SUSAN

How many times have I told you to bring a complete set on each trip?

TOM

Don't tell me how to run my business.

CUT TO:

INT. FATHER'S STUDY – DAY

It is a messy study with papers and books and video samples everywhere – stacked on the floor, on shelves, on top of a TV set. RAY *rummages around behind the desk through stacks of sample video covers.*

CUT TO:

INT. SUSAN'S BEDROOM – DAY

RAY *walks in.* SUSAN *still talks on the phone.*

SUSAN

If you ran your business right you wouldn't have to travel all the time, would you? The guys who make the money let other people travel for them.

TOM

I like to travel. What's the matter with traveling?

She hands the phone up for RAY, *who take it.*

CUT TO:

INT. MOTEL – DAY

The WOMAN *sits on the bed next to* TOM *and starts reading a magazine.*

RAY

Dad?

TOM

She stays home and critiques my life while I'm out here trying to earn a living. Does that seem fair to you?

RAY *is silent.*

Did you find the samples?

> RAY
> (*off screen*)

No.

> TOM

Shit. Did you look behind the desk?

> RAY

Yes.

> TOM

You've got to find them.

RAY *says nothing. He looks scared.*

Did you hear me?

> RAY

Yes.

> TOM

You haven't touched the car, have you?

> RAY

No.

> TOM

And you're taking good care of the dog?

> RAY

The dog seems fine.

> TOM

How about the teeth?

> RAY

What?

> TOM

Are the gums red and bleeding?

                              RAY

No.

                              TOM

Please find the samples, Ray.

                              RAY

But I can't find them.
  CUT TO:

INT. SUSAN'S BEDROOM – DAY

RAY *holds the phone loosely in his hand and looks helplessly at his mother. She takes it from his hand and hangs it up.*

                         AUNT HELEN

Look how big he's getting.

  SUSAN *says nothing.*

And handsome, too. He'll be fighting off the girls soon.

                            SUSAN
                           (*dully*)

It's already started.

  They say nothing.

                         AUNT HELEN

But he'll have to learn to be more precise with time if he's going to be the first doctor in the family.

  RAY *starts to leave.*

Where are you going?

                              RAY

Out.

                         AUNT HELEN

As long as you're going to be here, I could use your help taking your mother to her doctor's appointment.

                              RAY

You take her.

SUSAN

Raymond.

RAY

I wasn't going to be here at all, was I?

AUNT HELEN

But you are, and we could certainly use your help.

RAY

I'm sure you can manage.

AUNT HELEN

He's probably got a girl to see.

RAY
(snaps)

I don't have a girl to see.

AUNT HELEN

He's at that age.

RAY

Helen, do me a favor and shut your big fat mouth.

AUNT HELEN *is shocked.*

AUNT HELEN

He's got Tom's temper, doesn't he?

SUSAN
(frustrated)

Helen, you're only making things worse, now please shut up.

Pause, AUNT HELEN *looks hurt and tearful.*

AUNT HELEN

I have not liked the way I have been treated since the minute I stepped into this house. I left a husband, two cats, and a summer garden to help you out, and if this is the thanks I get, you can just take care of yourself.

She leaves the room. RAY *stands there for a moment, then bolts after her.*

CUT TO:

234

EXT. DRIVEWAY — DAY

AUNT HELEN *walks to her car with her little suitcase while* RAY *chases her.*

> RAY
>
> I'm sorry, I swear to God, please don't go.

> AUNT HELEN
>
> You said I have a fat mouth.

> RAY
>
> You don't have a fat mouth. Wait.

She gets into her car and leaves him standing in the driveway.
CUT TO:

INT. RAY'S ROOM — DAY

He walks in, seething with rage, and he doesn't know what to do. He takes his suitcase, throws it against the wall, and tears down his science posters.
CUT TO:

INT. BATHROOM — DAY

RAY *walks in and closes the door. He looks at himself in the mirror and looks nauseous, depressed.*

RAY *takes the bottle of aspirin from the cabinet, takes the top off, and accidentally spills the aspirin all over the sink. He picks a few out of the sink and chews them as he looks at his bloated face in the mirror.*

He turns the shower on and gets in with his clothes on. The shower pours onto his head and he closes his eyes. He pulls his wet clothes off, and picks up a small cleaning brush that's on the floor, and scrubs his skin with it.

He turns the shower off, gets out, and brushes his teeth furiously, looking in the mirror. He rinses and begins again, brushing his teeth a second time. He looks at himself in the mirror, depressed.

CLOSE UP: RAY'S *hand reaches for the soap in the shower.*
CUT TO:

RAY *scrubs himself with a brush in the shower.*
   CUT TO:

INT. SUSAN'S BEDROOM – DAY

She sits up in the big bed, looking straight ahead, sad.
   CUT TO:

INT. RAY'S BATHROOM – DAY

RAY *turns the shower on again.*
   CUT TO:

CLOSE UP: *He reaches for the soap in the shower.*
   CUT TO:

INT. SUSAN'S BEDROOM – DAY

SUSAN *sits, looking at her face in a small mirror she holds, touching the circles under her eyes.*
   CUT TO:

INT. RAY'S BATHROOM – DAY

RAY *towels himself off, when he hears the dog scratching at the door. He looks annoyed.*
   CUT TO:

INT. KITCHEN – DAY

RAY, *nude, drags the dog by the collar across the kitchen linoleum and throws him out the door.*
   CUT TO:

INT. SUSAN'S BEDROOM – DAY

               SUSAN
              (lies in bed)
Raymond.

   He doesn't answer.

Raymond.

He ignores her.

I have to get ready for my appointment.

RAY *appears in the doorway with a towel around his waist and looks at his mother.*

What happened to your skin? You've got such lovely skin and you've rubbed it raw.

                              RAY
Do me a favor and don't worry about it.

                              SUSAN
How do you expect me to get to town?

                              RAY
Call a taxi.

Pause

                              SUSAN
                            (*quietly*)
I'm not going to call a taxi.
     CUT TO:

INT. SUSAN'S BATHROOM – DAY

RAY *stands with the towel wrapped around his waist outside the shower curtain while his mother holds onto his arm with one hand and showers inside.*
     CUT TO:

INT. SUSAN'S BEDROOM – DAY

RAY, *dressed in jeans and a faded Oxford, zips his mother into a very flattering white summer dress.*
     CUT TO:

RAY *puts a white sandal onto her one good foot. He stands and looks at her a moment; she looks terrific.*
     CUT TO:

INT. GARAGE – DAY

RAY *pulls a big tarp off the cream-colored Lincoln.*
   CUT TO:

EXT. DRIVEWAY – DAY

The car idles in the driveway under a sunny clear sky as RAY *carries* SUSAN *in her summer dress to the car.* RAY *walks around and gets into the car.*

> SUSAN

Shit, here comes Walter Hooten.

> *A* MALE NEIGHBOR, *about fifty, with a tennis racquet approaches the car.* SUSAN *puts on a fake smile.*

Hello, Walter, how's it going?

> NEIGHBOR

I thought you might want to know I saw your dog head into the woods behind my house.

> SUSAN

Thank you, Raymond will look for him later, but right now we're late for an appointment.

> NEIGHBOR

Don't let me hold you up. Taking good care of your mother, Raymond?

> RAY *does not acknowledge the man at all, but stares straight ahead.*

You tell your Dad he should slow down and smell the roses. If I were him, I'd get myself a cigarette boat and some water skis –

> RAY *punches the gas as he backs out of the driveway.*

Don't let me hold you up.
   CUT TO:

EXT. COUNTRY ROAD – DAY

RAY *drives the car through the quasi-rural suburb;* SUSAN *sits in the passenger seat.*
    CUT TO:

EXT. BREWSTER – DAY

A small town. RAY *carries his mother down the sidewalk, past pedestrians.*

                    PASSING WOMAN
Hi.

                        SUSAN
Hi. Judy.
    CUT TO:

INT. DOCTOR'S OFFICE – DAY

RAY *sits in a chair.* FRAN, *a mother like* SUSAN *with a son about* RAY*'s age, sits next to them in the little waiting room.* FRAN *wears casual gardening clothes, while her son wears jeans, T-shirt, and sneakers, making him look much younger than* RAY. *He has a cast on his right arm. While the mothers talk, the boys flip through magazines uncomfortably.*

                        FRAN
How are you?

                        SUSAN
Hanging in there. I get my crutches today.

                        FRAN
We're shopping for shoes. You know what that's like.

                        SUSAN
God. Is he as picky as Raymond?

                        FRAN
What do you think? If he had his way, he'd wear sneakers all year 'round. But he is not about to wear sneakers to his sister's wedding.

SUSAN

Don't I know it.

FRAN

He's strictly into that horrendous grunge thing.

RAY
(*loudly*)
What kind of shoes do you like to see on a guy, Fran?

SUSAN

'Fran?!'

RAY

I'm sure you've got a preference –

SUSAN

'Mrs Gibson', to you.

FRAN

He's too much, isn't he?

RAY

I'll tell you a funny story about shoes –

SUSAN

Will you lower your voice?

He leans over and speaks in a naughty undertone.

RAY

It was at Jones Beach. This short chunky guy with pale skin comes walking down the beach wearing a bathing suit, black shoes, and black socks, and he's got the biggest damn feet you ever saw in your life, I mean gun boats –

SUSAN

Raymond –

RAY

And he walks up and sits down next to these two beautiful girls in bikinis, and I'm thinking, 'Gee, maybe there's some correlation between shoe size –

SUSAN
(*snaps*)

That's enough.

He sit back, chastened. FRAN *and her son are looking at him with their mouths open.*

NURSE
(*smiling*)

Mrs Aibelli? The doctor will see you now.

DISSOLVE TO:

A large round clock on the wall of the waiting room.

DISSOLVE TO:

RAY *sits next to* FRAN *and her son in the waiting room, reading a magazine. They don't speak. The door opens and the* DOCTOR, *a suntanned man of about sixty-five, escorts* SUSAN *out on her new crutches.*

DOCTOR

Now try to move around every day, the healing process needs some help. You should've picked these crutches up a week ago, Raymond. Apparently your mother likes to spend too much time in the horizontal position. God, what am I saying?

He and SUSAN *laugh.* RAY *throws down the magazine and stands up, rolling his eyes. He takes his mother's arm from the* DOCTOR, *who holds the door open.*

The point is, with legs as pretty as yours, I'd hate to see this break heal in a bad way.

SUSAN
(*giggles*)

Stop it, Roger.

DOCTOR

Hey, Mom was just telling me about that internship.

SUSAN

He was very impressed, Raymond.

241

DOCTOR

You know, I'd be glad to write a general letter of recommendation for any of your endeavours.

SUSAN

Isn't that great?

DOCTOR

I remember when I was in your shoes.

RAY

Shoes? I've got a great story about shoes. I was at Jones Beach and –

SUSAN

Raymond will call you this week.

CUT TO:

INT. TOM'S LINCOLN – DAY

RAY *gets into the driver's seat and slams the door.* SUSAN *sits in the passenger seat.*

SUSAN

What was that ridiculous business with the shoes, for God's sake?

RAY

Fran brought it up.

SUSAN
(*shouts*)

Stop calling her Fran.

RAY

He said you should've had crutches, just like I told you.

SUSAN

That's enough. Just drive the car.

RAY *pulls out.*

CUT TO:

INT. KITCHEN – DAY

SUSAN *licks her finger and flicks the page of a science magazine as she sits at the table.* RAY *stands, talking on the phone, with the yellow pages open before him.*

> RAY
> (*on phone*)

Yes, she has a cast on her leg. She needs help bathing, getting around the house, right. Groceries. No, nothing medical, really except some medication.

He waits.

Don't you have anyone before then?

He looks disappointed.

Thanks.

He hangs up.
CUT TO:

CLOSE UP: *Yellow pages as* RAY *scans with his finger.*
CUT TO:

SUSAN *glances up from her magazine.* RAY *dials the phone. CUS: Pencil, yellow pages,* SUSAN *reads, turns magazine page.*
CUT TO:

> RAY
> (*on phone*)

Actually, I was hoping for someone tomorrow. Would you know any place that would have someone to start today or tomorrow? No, that's all right. Thanks.

He hangs up.

> SUSAN

I told you to wait until Monday.

> RAY

I'd like to go this weekend.

> SUSAN

You should've thought of that before you insulted your aunt.

> RAY

I wouldn't be here at all if you hadn't taken those pills.

SUSAN

Jeez, don't use that against me.

RAY

Then don't tell me I missed my train because I insulted Helen,
because that's bullshit.

SUSAN

Not entirely.

*He sits down, frustrated, and spills some salt on the table. He then
tries to balance the salt shaker on the edge of its bottom in the spilled
salt.*

Medical Mind started ten minutes ago. Do you want to watch it
with me?

RAY

No.

He keeps trying to balance the salt shaker.

SUSAN

Will you stop that? You're making a mess.

RAY

Why don't we call Mrs Brenner?

SUSAN

She's at the Cape.

He keeps trying to balance the salt shaker; it keeps spilling.

Why don't you want to watch *Medical Mind*?

RAY

Because I don't feel like watching one of your stupid science
shows, OK?

SUSAN

Since when are they *my* science shows?

RAY

They've always been *your* science shows.

Don't talk to me that way, and stop doing that.

He ignores her and continues to try to balance the salt shaker. She stands up with difficulty on her crutches and walks over to him. She grabs the wrist of his hand with the salt shaker, but he pulls it away. One of her crutches drops to the floor and she hangs on his arm. Her other crutch drops to the floor. She leans into him as he holds her by her wrists. Finally, he catches her around the waist and pulls her tight, into him. Their faces are close together and he lowers her to the floor.

What are you doing?

He looks down at her.

RAY

I'm going out for a while.

SUSAN

Wait a minute, help me up.

RAY

Bye.

SUSAN

Help me up, you son of a bitch.

He starts to go. She shrieks after him.

SUSAN
(screams)

Raymond, you bastard.

RAY
(on his way out)

Son of a bitch was more accurate.

CUT TO:

INT. TOM'S LINCOLN – DAY

RAY *drives along a back road.*

CUT TO:

EXT. FIELD — DAY

RAY *stands near the gazebo, whistling and shouting for the dog.*

RAY
Here, boy. Frank! Frank!

TONI *approaches in the distance behind him as he calls for the dog.*

TONI
How did you lose him?

He is surprised as he turns to look at her.

RAY
Did you have to tell your father every goddamn detail about what we did?

TONI
I was mad at you.

RAY
He called my mother.

She looks remorseful.

TONI
You're right. I shouldn't have told him.

RAY
Then why did you?

TONI
Because you got so rough.

RAY
You didn't like anything I did.

TONI
I thought you were acting weird.

RAY
What's weird? How many people have you kissed?

TONI
I don't know. How many people have you kissed?

Silence.

I'm sorry if I made you feel like there's something wrong with you.

                              RAY

There's nothing wrong with me. But I think there's something wrong with you if you have to go home and tell your father God knows what about me –

                              TONI

I was scared, OK?

    She looks at him.

I thought you were supposed to be in Washington.

                              RAY

My aunt couldn't stay.

                              TONI

What a drag.

    She looks at him as he stands there in the wind.

What are you gonna do?

                              RAY

I don't fucking know. I wish I could erase this life and start over.

    She watches his face and puts her hand to his cheek. Then she hugs
    him. He looks uncomfortable but slowly puts his arms around her.
    After a moment, they look at each other and start kissing.
    CUT TO:

    He lies on top of her on the grass. They are kissing.
    CUT TO:

    EXTREME LONG SHOT *across field:* RAY *lies on top of* TONI *on the*
    grass.
    CUT TO:

    He awkwardly pulls her pants down. He looks uncomfortable and
    stops. Pauses. Then he pulls her pants back up and sits next to her,
    not looking at her. She looks at his back and puts a hand on his

shoulder. He lies back and they lie side by side, not touching, not looking at each other.
DISSOLVE TO:

WIDE SHOT *of field: Night has fallen.*
DISSOLVE TO:

INT. FIELD – NIGHT

They still lie side by side.

                              RAY
Did you ever think about that?

                              TONI
No.

                              RAY
I bet you've thought about it.

   She thinks.

                              TONI
Maybe once.

                              RAY
When?

                              TONI
My parents sent me to camp and I drowned in the lake and everyone was crying at my funeral.

                              RAY
That's pretty good. I never thought about drowning.

                              TONI
What do you think about?

                              RAY
Phil Ochs hung himself with a belt over a door. He made a loop in the belt and put it around his neck. Then he put the end of the belt over the top of the door and closed it.

                              TONI
Who's Phil Ochs?
CUT TO:

INT. TOM'S LINCOLN – NIGHT

RAY *pulls up to* TONI*'s driveway, and they sit in the car looking straight ahead without saying anything for a moment.*

> TONI

When do you think you'll leave?

> RAY

As soon as we get a nurse.

> *She turns to him and he kisses her on the mouth. Then she opens the door and runs up her driveway in the dark.*
> CUT TO:

EXT. AIBELLI HOUSE – NIGHT

RAY *pulls the Lincoln into the driveway.*
> CUT TO:

INT. AIBELLI HOUSE – NIGHT

He walks in the kitchen door and goes to the refrigerator. He takes out a soda and an apple and walks through the dark hall to the den, where he jumps in fear, dropping the soda.

RAY*'s father sits on the sofa watching TV with his tie loosened and a beer in his hand.*

> TOM

How's it going, Ray?

> RAY

What are you doing here?

> TOM

I live here, don't I?

> TOM *stares at the TV as he talks.*

So you leave your mother alone for half the night?

> TOM *stands up.*

> RAY

No.

                              TOM

It's three in the morning, isn't it?

                              RAY

I don't know.

                              TOM

Was it an emergency?

   RAY *doesn't answer.*

I assume it was an emergency because that's the only reason you'd
use my car.

   RAY *remains silent.*

I found out Helen was here. I thought that was pretty interesting. I
don't like to have her in my house.

                              RAY

I know.

                              TOM

Then what was she doing here?

                              RAY

So I could go to Washington.

                              TOM

Speak up, I can't hear you.

                              RAY

I was going to Washington.

                              TOM

Wonderful. Leave your mother with Aunt Helen, what do you
care? Just look out for number one, right?

   He picks up a stack of video tape samples.

And look what I found.

                              RAY

I swear, I couldn't find them.

TOM

Now I've got to fly back first thing in the morning.

RAY

You came back just for those?

TOM

How do you think the bills get paid around here? By your prestigious summer job?

He throws the video samples onto the couch.

Now I believe we've got a very disturbing matter to discuss.
CUT TO:

EXT. MARSH – NIGHT

TOM *trudges through the muddy reeds, holding a flashlight.* RAY *looks exhausted as he walks through the wet mud behind his father.*

TOM
(calls)

Frank! Here boy.
CUT TO:

EXT. FIELD – NIGHT

They walk across a field.

TOM
(calls)

Frank! Here boy.
CUT TO:

EXT. WOODS – NIGHT

TOM *walks in the lead with the flashlight, looking for the dog.* RAY *looks drained as they go through some bushes.* TOM *calls and whistles for the dog.*
CUT TO:

EXT. WOODS – NIGHT

They sit, exhausted, defeated, muddy.

251

TOM

Lou Vacarro gave me that dog. He went to Australia to sell the discount chains, fell in love with these pups, half Rhodesian Ridgebacks. He went to the trouble to bring one back for me, because I gave him some beautiful product he sold the hell out of. I think he did a hundred thousand units. I know you and your mother don't think much of my work.

RAY

That's not true.

TOM

Come on, I know the score.

RAY

We wish you didn't have to travel so much.

TOM *stops and looks at* RAY.

TOM

That's the name of the game in sales, and I never regretted it. Sometimes I think I missed not seeing more of what's going on with you. I was thinking we could maybe work together a little. You'd be great for the business.

RAY
(*awkwardly*)
Thanks . . . I don't know if I'd be that good at it.

TOM

This business trip has been a disaster so far. I don't know what the fuck is happening to the video market. (*Pause*) I hate to tell you this, I don't think I can afford next year's tuition, with or without the loans and scholarships.

Pause.

RAY

Is that definite?

TOM

It's not the end of the world, at least I hope not. You'll have to spend the year at home and earn some money. That's why I thought we could try working together.

252

Suddenly the dog comes bounding out of the brush and jumps up on
TOM, *wagging his tail furiously.* TOM *looks very happy.*

Look at that, will you? Doesn't look any worse for the wear, does
he?
> (*speaks to the dog*)

I was worried about you, yes I was, yes I was, good boy, thatta
boy.

RAY *watches sadly while his father plays with the dog and inspects
the dog's teeth.*

Check him for any cuts or abrasions. A dog should always have a
wet nose, did you know that? Now his nose is a little dry, which
leads me to think he might be dehydrated.

RAY *stares at his father. Then turns and walks away.*
CUT TO:

INT. SUSAN'S BEDROOM – DAY

SUSAN *sits in bed reading with her glasses on while* TOM *walks back
and forth, putting stacks of sample tapes into a sales case; the dog
follows him back and forth.*

> TOM

How's your leg?

> SUSAN

Still sore.

*He sits on the opposite side of the bed from her as she continues to
stare at the TV.*

> TOM

How sore?

> SUSAN

It wakes me up most nights.

*He reaches his hand over and tentatively touches her thigh above the
cast. She stares at the TV. He withdraws his hand. Then he leans
over slowly, awkwardly, to give her a peck on the cheek just as she
starts coughing. He freezes, watching her cough, then she turns to the*

253

nightstand, drinks from her glass, and takes a pill. She resumes her
position watching the TV. He reaches forward carefully and strokes
her hair, putting it behind her ear. He touches her cheek as she
watches the TV. He looks at her a moment, then gets up and goes
back to his samples.
CUT TO:

INT. KITCHEN – DAY

RAY *sits eating his breakfast across from* SUSAN *and* TOM.

TOM

Maybe when your leg gets better, we could take a little trip to the
Berkshires. Spend some time together.

SUSAN

Can we afford it?

TOM

You know, I've been thinking of a way to get out of this hole we're
in. I mentioned it to Ray last night.

She looks at him. He gives the dog a scrap of food.

SUSAN

Tom.

TOM

I know, but he's been in the woods for a few days. He deserves it.

SUSAN

What was your idea?

TOM

If he came on as a salesman, I could probably double what I'm
doing now.

SUSAN

He doesn't want to go into the business with you, Tom. He wants
to be a doctor.

TOM

OK, I have no problem with that. Why can't he be a salesman now
and a doctor later? He's young.

254

SUSAN

There has to be a way for him to go back to school this fall.

TOM

I'll gladly show you the numbers. They just don't add up.

TOM *resumes eating his breakfast.*

Hey, you know who I ran into at the convention? Art Sackheim, do you remember him, Ray? Tall guy with freckles all over his head, always giving out little wind-up toys?
CUT TO:

EXT. DRIVEWAY – DAY

TOM *leaves in his cream-colored Lincoln.*
CUT TO:

INT. KITCHEN – DAY

SUSAN *stands speaking on the phone while* RAY *watches.*

SUSAN

That would be terrific. Yes, maybe next year, if you'd just hold the internship open for him.

She listens and laughs.

Tell me about it. I've been a reader of your journal since it started, and it still took three years to get the library where I work to subscribe. OK, I've gotta go, too. Thanks so much. I will.

She hangs up. RAY *sits there while* SUSAN *clears the plates, with some difficulty, on her crutches.*

She stops at the sink and looks at him. He looks devastated.

She's going to hold the spot open until you can go, even if it takes a year. She asked you to submit some new essays.

RAY

I don't feel like starting anything new.

SUSAN

Take a little time. You need a break.

She opens a bottle of pills on the kitchen counter, takes two, and swallows them with a glass of water, then looks at him sympathetically.
    CUT TO:

INT. DEN — DAY

In the darkened den, SUSAN *and* RAY *sit side by side on the sofa while they watch TV.*
    CUT TO:

TV SCREEN: *A DNA model is reviewed by a doctor.*
    CUT TO:

SUSAN *puts her leg up on the sofa and leans into* RAY's *arms. She gets comfortable there. She sleeps in his lap while they watch TV.*
    CUT TO:

TV SCREEN: *A man smiles and laughs while describing the DNA model.*
    DISSOLVE TO:

LATER: *She lies asleep in* RAY's *lap. The doorbell rings.* RAY *gets up very carefully, putting a pillow under her head so she doesn't stir.*
    CUT TO:

INT. FRONT DOOR — DAY

RAY *opens the door and finds* TONI *there.*

                              TONI
Hi.

                              RAY
I told you not to come over here.

                              TONI
I want to talk to you.

                              RAY
This is a bad time.

                              TONI
Why can't I come to your house? Is it because I'm too young?

                              RAY

No. We'll talk later.

                              TONI

But I want to talk now. Show me your room.

                              RAY

My mother's sleeping.

                              TONI

I'll be very quiet.
   CUT TO:

INT. RAY'S ROOM – DAY

They walk silently in, and RAY *carefully closes the door. He stands by
the unmade bed while* TONI *walks around, inspecting the room. She
examines the torn posters, the ripped up papers, the computer thrown in
the corner.*

                              TONI

Is it always this messy?

                              RAY

Not really.

   He makes a lame effort to pick up a few things.

                              TONI

What's happening with the internship?

                              RAY

I don't feel like thinking about it.

                              TONI

How come?

   He watches as she picks up a picture of RAY*'s family.*

Is this your mother?

                              RAY

Yes.

                              TONI

She's pretty. Don't you think?

                              RAY

No.

    He takes the picture and puts it face down.

                              TONI

Are you in another bad mood?

    She sits on the bed.

                              RAY

Maybe we could get together sometime tomorrow, OK?

                              TONI

What's the matter?

                              RAY

I can't go back to school this year. We can't afford it.

    *She picks up a wooden box and opens it. She looks through his little
    things inside.*

                              TONI

Look at the bright side: we can hang out for a year while I finish
high school, and if I get into MIT, we'll both go back together.

    He takes the box and puts it down.

                              RAY,

I showed you my room, now I think you should go. I'll call you
later.

                              TONI

I want to talk about our sex.

                              RAY

Why?

                              TONI

My friend Kim says it's OK if you need to go slower, but guys
think they're not supposed to do that.

                              RAY
                           (*agitated*)

Who's Kim?

TONI

My best friend. I never told you about Kim?

RAY

No, you never told me about Kim.

She takes his hands and starts dancing slowly.

TONI

Yes, I did. You never listen to me.

RAY

Toni, what are you doing?

They keep dancing without music, until she dances back to the bed and sits.

You really should go.

TONI
(*holding his hand*)

I don't want to go, come on.

He looks at her for a moment.

RAY

Wait.

He grabs a chair and puts it in front of the door to hold it shut, then he puts an ear to the door and listens. He turns on his tape player, but not too loud. Then he sits next to her on the bed. They sit this way for a moment. Then she kisses him softly on the cheek. Then the mouth. He starts to kiss her aggressively, but she stops him.

TONI

Slow down.

He looks at her awkwardly. She slowly kisses his neck while he looks uncomfortable. They kiss gently.

(*smiling*)

Isn't this nice?

They take their shirts off. Continue to kiss. Suddenly the door explodes open. SUSAN stands in the doorway on her crutches. She looks druggy and dark, out of breath. They are frozen with fear. No one says anything. TONI *covers her chest with her hands.*

SUSAN

I asked you not to do this, Raymond.

TONI

We're not doing anything.

TONI *puts her shirt on.*

SUSAN

Shouldn't you be home studying for the SAT's or something?

TONI

I don't see why Raymond can't have me over to his house.

SUSAN *walks up to them on her crutches.*

SUSAN

Oh, Raymond can have you over to his house, he just can't fuck you in his house, though I don't know why he'd want to after all the trouble you caused him.

RAY *stands as* TONI *sits on the bed, fixing her hair.*

RAY

That's enough. She's going.

TONI
(*to* SUSAN)

I don't know how you can have so much inappropriate control over his life.

SUSAN
(*to* RAY)

Is this how you like them? Little baby psycho-talk.

RAY

At least she's not old and pathetic.

SUSAN *swings her open hand at* RAY *just as* TONI *stands up between them and accidentally takes the full blow.* TONI *falls to the floor, holding her left eye with one hand.* SUSAN *looks at* TONI, *upset and contrite.*

SUSAN

Honey, I'm sorry.

TONI *gets up and runs from the house, crying.*

RAY

You make me sick.

She swings at RAY *and hits him once across the face, then swings
again. He catches her by the wrist and throws her down to the bed.
They wrestle and hit on the bed. He manages to throw her on her
back. He rips her shirt open, exposing her bra. She holds her arms
above her head and smiles as he falls on her.*
FADE OUT:

FADE IN – INT. KITCHEN – DAY

CLOSE UP: *A hamburger flips on the griddle.*
CUT TO:

SUSAN *stands humming happily in the kitchen wearing another pair of
shorts and* RAY*'s old striped Oxford shirt while she cooks hamburgers at
the stove. Her hair is pulled back in a youthful pony tail.*

                              SUSAN
                       (calling to another room)
Honey, do you want a beer with this?
     CUT TO:

INT. DEN — NIGHT

RAY *sits on the couch watching TV. He shouts back at her.*

                              RAY
Sure.

     The doorbell rings.

                              SUSAN
                          (off screen)
I'll get it.
     CUT TO:

INT. FRONT DOOR — DAY

SUSAN *walks on crutches to the front door using one crutch. When she opens it, she faces* DR PECK, TONI*'s father. He has his arm around* TONI, *who wears a white eye patch over her left eye.*

                          DR PECK
Mrs Aibelli?

                          SUSAN
Yes.

                          DR PECK
Did you do this to my daughter?

                          SUSAN
I can hardly imagine –

                          DR PECK
Did you or did you not hit my daughter?

                          SUSAN
Is that what she told you?

                            TONI
It's true.

                              262

DR PECK

Do you have any idea how painful a scratched cornea can be?

She stares at him.

SUSAN

Why don't you come in and we'll discuss exactly what happened.

CUT TO:

INT. KITCHEN – DAY

SUSAN *sits facing* DR PECK *and* TONI *across the table.*

SUSAN

Let's get one thing straight. Your daughter was in my son's room with her shirt off.

DR PECK

The sex doesn't concern me.

SUSAN

Why are psychologists always such permissive parents?

DR PECK

Toni and I have talked about sex. I'm confident she knows what she's doing. Do you realize you could be facing a lawsuit, Mrs Aibelli?

SUSAN

A lawsuit? You must be kidding –

DR PECK

You assaulted my daughter.

SUSAN

I guess that would make the summer complete. I break my leg. Tom goes on another business trip. Raymond skips his internship. I find these two humping in my house, and now I've got a lawsuit.

DR PECK

I'm not here to discuss your personal problems.

She grows more emotional.

SUSAN

What would you like to discuss? Do you think I'm some kind of a monster? I know I lost my temper. I'm not a very happy woman right now. If that's a crime, then go ahead and sue me. I'm sorry I hit your daughter, it was an accident. I was angry at Raymond and she stepped in the way.

Her eyes get teary. She reaches out and touches TONI*'s face.*

I never intended to hurt her.

TONI *recoils from* SUSAN*'s touch.*

DR PECK

Wait outside.

TONI *gets up and leaves.* DR PECK *looks at* SUSAN *with a glimmer of compassion.*

SUSAN

My doctor has me on so much medication I don't know if I'm coming or going.

DR PECK *hands her his handkerchief.*

Thank you.

She wipes her eyes and blows her nose.

DR PECK

What kind of medication?

SUSAN

Darvocet for the pain in my leg. Zoloft for depression.

DR PECK

There's so much irresponsible prescribing today. Do you have an analyst?

SUSAN

Do you think that's worthwhile? Of course you do, you're a psychiatrist. What a stupid question . . . I'm sorry, I haven't even offered you anything to drink.

DR PECK

Iced tea is fine.

She struggles to get up.

Let me get it.

He gets up, takes a glass from the cabinet, and pours himself iced tea at the table.

How long have you been on the Zoloft?

SUSAN

It started last year. Tom travels so much, and now Raymond's gone.

DR PECK

It sounds like you're alone a lot.

SUSAN

I'm alone a great deal of the time.

DR PECK

That can be very stressful. You were probably jealous of Toni and Ray.

SUSAN

What did you say your first name was, doctor?

DR PECK

Henry.

CUT TO:

INT. DEN – NIGHT

RAY *slouches in depressed silence, staring into the television.* TONI *walks in and sits down in a chair.* RAY *sits up.*

RAY

Are you OK?

She stares at the TV.

TONI

The cornea is scratched.

RAY

I'm sorry, but I told you not to come over here.

TONI

Don't you even care what happened to me?

RAY

Of course I care.

TONI

So what did you do when I left?

He stares at the TV.

Did you say anything to her?

He looks at her.

Are you going to talk to me about this?

RAY

No.

TONI

I'm getting a little tired of your evasiveness.

RAY

I'm getting a little tired of your pushiness.

TONI

You're the one who does everything your parents want, not me.

RAY

Shut up.

TONI

You don't even know why you want to be a doctor, do you?

RAY

Am I paying for this session?

TONI

Cut it out. There's no reason why we can't talk about these things.

RAY

Yes, there is. You're not my girlfriend.

266

She leaves.
CUT TO:

INT. KITCHEN – NIGHT

> DR PECK
> (*laughing*)

No, it's quite common, actually. We're old and over the hill, they're young and just starting. Who wouldn't be jealous?

> SUSAN

Put another nail in the coffin, Henry.

> DR PECK

Don't bury me yet. I might have a few good years left in these legs.

> SUSAN

I'm down to one leg, but I'm still kicking.

> DR PECK

It's hard to imagine that your husband wouldn't want to stay home with you more of the time.

> SUSAN

Do me a favor and come over when he's back and let him know, would you?

> DR PECK
> (*laughs*)

My wife travels a lot, too.

> SUSAN

What does she do?

> DR PECK

She's an actress.

> SUSAN

She must be very pretty.

> DR PECK

Cathy's done quite well. It's always summerstock here or a commercial there. She's always going some place.

SUSAN

And you're a theater widow.

DR PECK

I guess you could put it that way.

SUSAN

We should have you and your daughter over to dinner sometime.
I'd be happy to cook for you.

DR PECK

That's very nice of you, but we better give Toni some time to calm
down.

SUSAN

I'm sure she'll get over it. They're a lot more resilient than we
think.

DR PECK

That's generally true.

SUSAN

How does this week look?
   CUT TO:

INT. DEN — NIGHT

RAY *sits watching TV alone. Off screen, he hears his mother's voice.*

SUSAN
(off screen)

Take care now, and don't forget to bring me that doctor's bill.

   The front door can be heard closing. After a moment, SUSAN *appears
   in the den on her crutches.*

He's certainly a nice man. Why didn't you tell me about him?

RAY

I don't know him.

SUSAN

Well, he's coming to dinner with Toni.

   RAY *stands up.*

RAY

No, he's not.

SUSAN

We haven't had company in ages, it could be just what we need to pick us up.

RAY

Are you out of your mind?

SUSAN

Don't start acting like your father. There is nothing wrong with wanting to have people over.

RAY

Does it occur to you that this might not be the best time to start entertaining again?

SUSAN

I don't see why not.

RAY

Maybe you can invite people into this house and pretend everything couldn't be better, but frankly I don't think I could handle it.

SUSAN

Try to see my side for once, Raymond.

RAY

I'm tired of seeing your side.

He pulls a folded paper from his back pocket and opens it: his father's itinerary.

SUSAN

What are you doing?

He picks up the phone.

RAY

We'll see how Dad feels about your side.

SUSAN

Don't do it.

He continues to dial.

He won't believe you.

He waits while the number rings on the other end.

We can handle this ourselves, Raymond.

> RAY
> *(into phone)*

I'd like to speak to Tom Aibelli, please.

> SECRETARY
> *(on phone)*

He's in a meeting with Mr Christopher.

> RAY

It's an emergency.

> RAY *waits. His mother stares at him.* TOM *speaks on a borrowed phone at a secretary's desk.*

> TOM
> *(to secretary)*

Thanks.

> *(into phone)*

Hello?

> RAY

It's Ray.

> TOM

I'm in a meeting.

> RAY

You've got to come home.

> TOM

Are you nuts? I just got back to Austin.

> RAY

It's an emergency.

> TOM

What's the big emergency?

RAY *is silent.*

Is it about your mother?

> RAY

Yes.

> TOM

Is she OK?

> RAY

No, she's not OK.

> TOM

Stop playing around. What happened?

RAY *pauses.*

> RAY

I can't stay here all year. I can't even stay here another day.

A business associate walks up to TOM.

> DEAN

Hey, big Tom Aibelli, how's it going?

> TOM

Hey, Dean. Long time, no see.

> DEAN

You playing much golf these days?

> TOM

Are you kidding? I'm working too hard.

> DEAN

That's no good. Let's hit the links while you're in town.

> TOM

I don't know, we'll see.
> *(back into phone)*

This won't change our financial situation, Ray. I still can't afford school next year.

> RAY

I know that.

TOM

Then don't try anything dramatic, because it won't work.

RAY

I don't care where I go, but I can't stay here.

TOM

Why?

Pause.

RAY

We're sleeping together.

TOM
(*off screen*)

Who?

RAY

Who do you think?

TOMS *turns to the secretary at the desk.*

TOM

Would you excuse me? It's a family matter.
              (*secretary leaves; he speaks into phone*)
Let me talk to your mother.

RAY

Why?

TOM
(*off screen*)

I want to find out what the hell is going on in my house, that's
why.

RAY

I'm telling you what's going on.

Pause. SUSAN *leaves the den on her crutches.*

TOM
(*off screen*)
You mother wouldn't do something that sick.

                              RAY
But I would?

                              TOM
                          (*off screen*)
I don't know what you're capable of, but I've been married to your
mother for over twenty years, and I think I know her a little better
than you do.

                              RAY
I don't believe this.

    SUSAN *picks up the extension.*

                            SUSAN
Hello?

                              TOM
Susan?

                            SUSAN
Tom?

                              TOM
What the hell is going on over there?

                            SUSAN
Why?

                              TOM
I don't even want to repeat what he said.

                            SUSAN
What did he say, Tom?

                              TOM
He said the two of you were sleeping together.

    There's another pause.

                            SUSAN
He's very upset about having to stay here.

                              TOM
Jesus, Raymond, what's the matter with you? This is crazy.

                              273

SUSAN

He doesn't want to be here, Tom. That's what it is.

RAY

Tell him the truth.

SUSAN

Hang up so I can talk to your father.

RAY

No. Tell him the truth.

SUSAN
(*off screen*)

Tom?

TOM
(*off screen*)

Yeah.

SUSAN
(*off screen*)

I'll call you later.

TOM
(*off screen*)

I really don't need this now. I'm in the middle of a real crisis here. Things are going very badly.

RAY

She has a birthmark on her ass, Dad, doesn't she?

TOM
(*off screen*)

Watch your mouth, Raymond.

RAY

The birthmark is shaped like a shopping cart, isn't it?

There's a pause on the line.

SUSAN
(*off screen*)

He must have seen it in the shower, Tom.

Another pause.

> TOM
> (*off screen*)

What the hell was he doing in the shower?

> SUSAN
> (*off screen*)

I need him to hold me up so I won't fall.

> TOM
> (*off screen*)

That's wonderful, Susan.

> SUSAN
> (*off screen*)

How do you expect me to shower with this cast? I fell a couple of days ago. If you were here –

> RAY

It wasn't just the shower, Dad.

> TOM
> (*off screen*)

Enough, Raymond. This is all because of that goddamned internship, isn't it?

> SUSAN
> (*off screen*)

Let me call you back.

> TOM
> (*off screen*)

Can you take care of this? Get him some help.

> SUSAN
> (*off screen*)

I'll try.

> TOM
> (*off screen*)

I really don't need this now. I'm in trouble as it is.

SUSAN
(*off screen*)
Don't worry, honey. I'll call you right back.

RAY

Don't hang up, Dad.

There's a pause.

TOM
(*off screen*)
Jesus.

TOM *hangs up. He looks concerned before he goes back to his meeting.* RAY *hangs up the phone. He walks slowly around the room and sits down, incredulous.*
CUT TO:

INT. DEN — NIGHT

RAY *sits in a daze.*
CUT TO:

INT. KITCHEN — NIGHT

RAY *comes in.*

RAY

You lied.

SUSAN

We don't have to drag your father into it.

RAY

How could he not be dragged into it?

Pause.

SUSAN
(*sympathetically*)
I know you're upset, but that's not the way to handle it . . . It's going to take time.

He looks at her dully and walks out of the kitchen.
CUT TO:

EMPTY HALL

EMPTY RAY'S BATHROOM

EMPTY SUSAN'S BEDROOM
CUT TO:

INT. KITCHEN – NIGHT

SUSAN *dumps the cold burgers in the garbage and puts new patties onto the griddle.*
CUT TO:

INT. LIVING ROOM – NIGHT

RAY *lies on the sofa, depressed. He gets up slowly and walks out.*

INT. HALLWAY – NIGHT

RAY *turns into the bathroom.*
CUT TO:

INT. RAY'S BATHROOM – NIGHT

He takes his belt off his pants.

RAY *makes a loop with a belt and puts the end of the belt over the top of the door. He closes the door so the belt forms a noose. He puts his head through the noose and lets his weight pull him down. His face turns red and he chokes.*

There is a brisk knock on the bathroom door.
CUT TO:

INT. HALLWAY – NIGHT

                              SUSAN
Hamburgers are ready.
CUT TO:

INT. BATHROOM – NIGHT

He looks like he is dead with his head hanging.

> SUSAN
> (*off screen*)

Come on, before they get cold.

He puts his feet down and catches his breath.

> RAY

In a minute.

> SUSAN
> (*off screen*)

I went to the trouble to make this, so get out here and eat it.

He puts the noose back on and hangs again. His face turns red, his breath grows raspy.

What's this belt sticking up in the door?

RAY stops hanging in order to reply.

> RAY
> (*irritably*)

Can't I do anything around here?

He hangs again for a moment. It looks like he'll die until she manages to open the door, and he falls to the floor, gasping. He glances up at her from the floor.

She holds onto the doorknob to lower herself onto the floor, where she leans on her side next to him.

> SUSAN

What are you doing to yourself?

She touches the red marks on his neck.

> RAY

Did I tell you I dreamed your cast was off last night?

> SUSAN

No, you didn't tell me.

He puts a hand on her thigh.

That sounds like a good dream.

She watches as he rubs her thigh. After a moment, she pushes his hand away. He puts his hand under her shirt again.

Stop it, honey.

After a pause, he pulls her down and kisses her hard. In the middle of the kiss, he puts his hands around her neck.

SUSAN
(*choking*)

Raymond –

He puts his strength into it. She pulls and scratches at his arms, but he squeezes her throat and chokes her. Her mouth opens speechlessly. Her eyes bulge. RAY *has a murderous look in his eyes as he continues to choke her while she struggles helplessly. It seems he will kill her.*

After a moment, her arms drop. She grows weak and is about to die.

Suddenly RAY *lets go. His mother convulses on the bathroom floor, coughs, and gasps for air.* RAY *sits on the floor while she lies there choking. When her choking subsides, she begins to weep.* RAY *takes her hand and holds it for a moment. Tears come to his eyes as he watches her cry.*

There is a sudden knocking at the curtained window above. A flashlight shines through.

NICKY

Raymond? Raymond? Listen, I'm sorry about the other night.

RAY *stands, looks at the window but doesn't say anything.*

What are you doing?

RAY

Choking my mother.

The boys break into laughter outside.

NICKY

Then I guess you better get out of the house.

CUT TO:

INT. NICKY'S CAR – NIGHT

The car flies along through the night. RAY *sits in the back seat between* DON *and* JOEL.

JOEL

Look who's here, Donnie.

DON

Tarzan, king of dicks.

A joint is passed to RAY *and he drags on it deeply and repeatedly.*

JOEL

Atta boy, Ray.

CURTIS

Looks like Popeye ate his spinach.
CUT TO:

EXT. NICKY'S CAR – NIGHT

Drives along the darkened semi-rural road.
CUT TO:

INT. NICKY'S CAR – NIGHT

CURTIS

First, take a hyperbolic paraboloid and a cone, and the paraboloid intersects the top of the cone, right? Now try to find the volume of the solid bounded by the cone and the hyperbolic paraboloid.

JOEL *and* DON *start laughing.* RAY *drinks a beer, numbed out.*

*[NICKY

You're stoned, Curtis.

CURTIS

I start with rectangular coordinates. Then I get stuck.

RAY

Switch to spherical coordinates.

*Cut from completed film

                              CURTIS
What are spherical coordinates?

                              NICKY
Whoa – what the fuck do we have here?
    CUT TO:

EXT. POV OF ROAD THROUGH NICKY'S WINDSHIELD – NIGHT

A girl rides a bicycle along the side of the road in the headlights of car.
CURTIS *rolls down his window.*

                              CURTIS
Hey, sweetheart, isn't it a little late for that sort of thing?

    NICKY *slowly cuts her off into some bushes.*

                              JOEL
Don't hit her, Nicky.

    *The car comes to a stop, and the girl is in the headlights with her
    back turned.*

                              DON
Leave her alone, man.

                              NICKY
Relax.

    The girl turns around, and it's TONI. *She has her white eye bandage
    on.*

                              RAY
Wait a minute, I know her.

                              CURTIS
You know her?

                              JOEL
I didn't know you knew any girls, Ray.

    RAY *climbs out of the car, followed by* CURTIS *and* NICKY.

EXT. ROAD – NIGHT

                    RAY
Toni.

                    TONI
What's going on?

                    RAY
He's just fooling around.

                    TONI
You scared me.

                    RAY
He's sorry.

                    NICKY
Yeah, I'm sorry.

                    RAY
What are you doing out here?

                    TONI
I was at Kim's.

    JOEL *opens a beer and sips it. They stand around in the headlights
    while rock plays on the radio.*

                    NICKY
Want a beer?

                    RAY
She doesn't want a beer.

                    TONI
Sure I do.

                    CURTIS
Wrong again, Ray.

    CURTIS *hands her a beer, which she opens and sips.*

                    NICKY
We're going swimming. Why don't you come?

                              RAY
They're not going swimming.

                              CURTIS
Yes, we are.

   TONI *hesitates.*

                              TONI
I'm not supposed to get my eye wet.

                              JOEL
We're experts at keeping eyes from getting wet.

                              RAY
This isn't for you, Toni.

                              TONI
How would you know?

                              NICKY
Yeah, Tarzan, how do you know?

                              TONI
What about my bike?

                              CURTIS
That's what trunks are for, honey.

                              TONI
Don't 'honey' me, asshole.

   She walks her bike to the trunk.

                              JOEL
Hey, she's all right.

   RAY *gets back into the car while* NICKY *opens the trunk.*

INT. NICKY'S CAR – NIGHT

                              CURTIS
Ray, you devil.

                              JOEL
Gonad the Nimrarian.

TONI *gets into the front and sits between* NICKY *and* CURTIS. *The car pulls out. They ride along. A joint is passed and* TONI *takes it.*

NICKY

I'm Nicky, and this is Curtis, Joel and Donnie.

CURTIS

How do you know Ray?

TONI

Through his dog.

CURTIS

His dog?

They crack up.

JOEL

The dog has all the personality in that family.

TONI

To tell you the truth, I don't really know him.

RAY

That's not true.

TONI

Yes it is, and he definitely doesn't know me.

NICKY

I think we have a communication problem here.

CURTIS

Where do you go to school?

TONI

Central. I've got another year.

NICKY

Jail bait.

Laughter.

TONI

Where do you guys go to school?

CURTIS

Joel and I go to Buffalo, Nick goes to Colgate, and Don is an Ivy League man.

TONI

Which Ivy school?

CURTIS

I think she's impressed, Don.

DON

Dartmouth.

TONI

Wow. I really want to go there.

DON

Really?

TONI

Do you like it?

DON

I love it.

JOEL

She's definitely impressed.

DON

You gonna come up for an interview?

TONI

Will you show me around?

DON

Sure.

JOEL

I wouldn't trust him. He raped all those girls in Florida last year.

DON

That's not funny, you asshole.

JOEL

They didn't think so, either.

                         DON
Don't be rude, shithead.

                         JOEL
Sorry, Mr Politeness.

                        NICKY
What about Colgate?

                         TONI
I don't know. It seems so nondescript.

                        CURTIS
Ouch. Later for you, Nicky.

                        NICKY
Wait a minute. What do you know about Colgate?

                         DON
She doesn't want to know about Colgate. She wants to know
about Dartmouth. What's your major going to be, Toni?

                        CURTIS
Do you know this problem with the hyperbolic paraboloid and the
cone?

                         JOEL
Not this again.

                         TONI
I'm not a math person.

                        NICKY
Ouch, Curtis. Looks like Don's her boy tonight.

   RAY *looks dead-eyed.*
   CUT TO:

EXT. GORGE – NIGHT

The car pulls up to some bushes under the trees and stops. NICKY *cuts
the engine and turns the radio off. They get out and stand around the
car drinking beer. The headlights are still on. They walk in the beams of
the headlights through some bushes to the edge of the quarry.*

TONI

Did you join a fraternity?

DON

Yeah. Theta Delta.

CURTIS

I think you better tell her about the special thing, Don.

DON

Right. The special thing.

TONI

What special thing?

DON

It's something you absolutely must know for college admissions.

TONI

What's that?

JOEL

That wouldn't be the PB thing, would it?

DON

As a matter of fact, I think it would.

TONI

PB. What's that?

DON

Pink belly.

He lunges at TONI, *but she throws her beer at him and runs away, screaming with laughter. Everyone but* RAY *chases her.* RAY *watches them disappear into the bushes and hears their shouts and* TONI's *shrieks.*

TONI

Wait. Stop it. I said stop! No!

They pull her shirt up.

It goes on until RAY *runs through the bushes and finds the boys huddled over* TONI. *He pushes them off of her one by one, knocking them over.*

Watch it, asshole.

CURTIS

Take it easy.

Everything stops. TONI *lies on the ground with her shirt up exposing her waist.*

RAY

She's only fifteen.

TONI

You're such an asshole, Raymond.

CURTIS

Truer words were never spoken.

RAY

Why are you acting like this?

TONI

Like what, mama's boy?

JOEL

Snap.

TONI

Have you met Ray's mother?

CURTIS

Yeah. Ray's mother is pretty hot.

JOEL
(*laughs*)

Curtis has a thing for Ray's mom.

TONI

She's a real witch.

NICKY

I'll bet.

TONI

She's the one who scratched my eye. She's got Ray right under her thumb.

RAY *doesn't say anything.* DON *picks* TONI *up and heaves her, shrieking, over his shoulder and walks off with her.*

CURTIS

I guess he's gonna show her Dartmouth.

RAY *stares after* TONI *and* DON.

JOEL
(*to* RAY)

I think she really likes you.

The others walk back toward the edge of the quarry.

CURTIS

That was fun. What should we do now, Ray?]*

CURTIS *sits down and takes a joint from* NICKY. *With a dull look in his eyes,* RAY *walks straight past them.*

SLOW MOTION: CURTIS *and* NICKY *blow pot smoke and watch* RAY *walk past.*

RAY*'s face, oddly intent, as he walks toward the edge.*

RAY*'s feet, as he walks.*

CURTIS *and* JOEL *go from laughing to scared as they watch.*

FROM BEHIND: RAY *jumps into the darkness.*

Still lifes of rocks below waiting in the water, various shots.

RAY *falling through the air.*

A baby in a swing outside.

A baby in the tub with SUSAN.

RAY *falling through air.*

The rocks below in still lifes.

A laughing boy of ten in the shower.

RAY*'s father looking serious.*

---

*In completed film the boys walk through the woods, then settle down on a rock.

RAY *gets his diploma.*

Quick refrain of empty rooms in the house.

Rocks below.

TONI *smiles.*

SUSAN *looks over her shoulder the night they slept together.*

NICKY, CURTIS, JOEL *look over the edge in horror.*

RAY *hits the water with a rush of sound.*

> NICKY

Holy shit. Where is he?

> JOEL

I don't know. I can't see him.

> NICKY *snaps his broken lighter repeatedly trying to light a joint.*

> CURTIS

What if something happened to him, Nicky?

> NICKY

Something did happen to him. And it's pretty bad.

> *They look at each other.* CURTIS *goes to the edge of the gorge and leans over.*

> CURTIS
> (*shouts into gorge*)

Hey. Asshole.

> *There is no answer.*

Raymond.

> *No answer.* CURTIS *looks at the others. He walks to the car and returns with a big flashlight which he shines down into the gorge.*
> CUT TO:

> POV FROM CLIFF: *The beam of the flashlight sweeps the black water of the deep gorge.*

CURTIS

Where the fuck is that asshole?

NICKY
(*shouts*)

Raymond. Raymond.

The boys look at each other. TONI *and* DON *emerge from the bushes; she puts her shirt back on.*

DON

What's going on?

CURTIS

Raymond jumped.

JOEL

We've got to find a way to get down there.

NICKY

You can't climb down these fucking cliffs.

JOEL

Then what should we do?

DON

Oh, my God. We have to call the police.

TONI *walks to the edge.*

TONI
(*shouts*)

Raymond. Raymond.

No answer. She starts to shake. DON *puts an arm around* TONI.

CURTIS

Raymond. If you can hear us, yell.

CUT TO:

EXT. GORGE WATER – NIGHT

The camera pans the dark surface of the water, past sharp rocks and logs.

One of RAY*'s sneakers floats into the frame. The camera continues to* *pan until it comes to a sharp rock jutting from the water.* RAY *clings to the rock, looking up toward the cliff where the others are.*

> CURTIS
> *(off screen)*

Raymond.

RAY smiles. He lets go, swims to the edge, and climbs out on some rocks. He is barefoot.

EXT. WOODS – NIGHT

He walks through the thick woods in his bare feet, stepping on twigs and roots, breaking branches. He crosses a stream. Bushes scratch his legs and his face.

CLOSE UP: *His scratched feet walk on the forest floor.*

He stops and listens to the sounds of the woods at night. Then he starts to walk.

> CUT TO:

RAY *comes out of the woods and onto a highway.*

EXT. HIGHWAY – NIGHT

RAY *stands in the scattered light of the oncoming traffic and sticks his thumb out. The cars zoom past him.*

After a moment, a big semi pulls to the side of the road. RAY *runs toward the red tail lights in the dark.*

> CUT TO:

INT. TRUCK – NIGHT

RAY *gets in. Country music plays. A crusty old* TRUCKER, *sixty, wearing glasses takes a look at* RAY.

> TRUCKER

What the fuck happened to you?

> RAY

I fell into an old quarry.

TRUCKER

A what?

RAY

An old quarry.

TRUCKER

Those are dangerous fucking places. You coulda been killed.

RAY *looks straight ahead, hugging his arms to his wet body.*

RAY

Yeah. I'm still in one piece.

The TRUCKER *gears back up and into traffic.*
DISSOLVE TO:
INT. SUSAN'S BEDROOM – NIGHT

CLOSE UP: SUSAN*'s sad face as she lies on her back, staring at the ceiling (and the camera) as the camera pulls up, through the ceiling, higher and higher, revealing her lonely figure on the bed.*
DISSOLVE TO:

INT. MOTEL ROOM – NIGHT

TOM *sits down and opens a beer on the motel bed, alone, watching TV.*
DISSOLVE TO:

EXT. HIGHWAY – NIGHT

The semi swings across the frame and disappears down the highway.
FADE TO BLACK.